Professional Integration:

A Guide for Students from the Developing World

Mary Ann G. Hood
Kevin J. Schieffer
Editors

Education for International Development
National Association for Foreign Student Affairs
Washington, D.C.   1983

The National Association for Foreign Student Affairs is a nonprofit membership association that provides training, information, and other educational services to professionals in the field of international educational exchange. The membership is composed of more than 4,500 representatives of postsecondary institutions, school systems, community organizations, and educational associations. Members implement Association programs and participate in the determination of policies and activities through their Board of Directors and more than 35 committees, commissions, and special interest groups.

Copies of this publication can be ordered from the Publications Order Desk, National Association for Foreign Student Affairs, 1860 19th Street, N.W., Washington, D.C. 20009.

Copyright ©1983 by National Association for Foreign Student Affairs. All rights reserved. Printed in the United States of America.

Library of Congress Catalog Card Number: 83-63519
ISBN: 0-912207-02-7

Contents

Preface v
    Martin Limbird

The Authors vii

1. Introduction 1
   Kevin J. Schieffer

2. Alumni Networking 5
   Kenneth A. Rogers

3. The Scientist or Scholar Interacts: Communication and Interpersonal Relations in the Developing Countries 25
   Michael J. Moravcsik

4. The Professional Integration of Women 47
   Mary Joy Pigozzi
   Patricia W. Barnes-McConnell
   Sally K. Williams

5. Research and Publication 70
   Motoko Y. Lee
   D.Y. Lee

6. Developing a Resource Library 105
   Harold Borko
   Eileen Goldstein

7. Continuing Education for the Returned Professional 124
   Stephen C. Dunnett

8. Conclusion 135
   Mary Ann G. Hood

Preface

An ever-present concern of the U.S. Agency for International Development (AID) is the timely professional reintegration of its U.S.-trained participants into their professional positions in their home countries. The development and publication of *Professional Integration: A Guide for Students from the Developing World,* in 1983, is both a confirmation of this concern and a reflection of the evolving role U.S. campus-based personnel are being asked to play in the process of the professional reintegration of students from the developing world. This collaborative approach has evolved rapidly over the past ten years, and the National Association for Foreign Student Affairs (NAFSA) has proved to be a key organization in helping campus personnel adapt and apply AID's field experience to the professional reintegration of returned students.

Ten years ago, I had the opportunity of observing AID's reintegration activities in Ghana. Under the inspired efforts of an AID training officer, returned participants were provided with information on existing networks made up of other AID-sponsored professionals, they were given publications of relevance to their particular fields, and they were invited to use the worldwide resources of AID. The training officer's efforts were complemented by those of the U.S. Information Agency's public information officer, who encouraged interaction among the returned graduates from all U.S. colleges and universities by providing publications, access to media equipment, and assistance in hosting alumni gatherings. An up-to-date directory of returned AID participants was available, chronicling the specific role in development played by each Ghanian student whom AID had sponsored. This network was not just a figment of the imagination of some U.S. government representatives; an informal study conducted among alumni of my own institution, Iowa State University, confirmed that they had used the network of U.S.-trained persons extensively in their contribution to the development of Ghana.

What was missing in this equation of professional reintegration, according to the alumni interviewed at that time in Ghana, was the recognition from the very beginning of the participants' sojourn in the United States of the need to prepare for return home. In other words, the faculty, the foreign student adviser, the community volunteer, and others needed to better understand the entire U.S. experience as part of a professional development continuum. What does it mean to be a "professional" in the development process? What are the professional's needs beyond the parameters of a standard degree program? What is the role of the professional in U.S. society beyond the world of work? How does that role con-

Preface

trast with the professional's role in the developing world? How can leadership skills be acquired to help the professional contribute more to the development process?

Members of NAFSA posed questions such as these to the AID Office of International Training beginning in 1973; these questions led to the funding of exemplary programs in civic participation activities, workshops in comparative leadership skills, publications on how to develop alumni networks, seminars on the relevance of the curriculum to students from the developing world, and a course on reentry-transition issues.

Assessment of the final reports of these projects and studies led the NAFSA/AID Steering Committee to the conclusion that these experiences needed to be formally addressed in book form. In this way, the benefits accrued from NAFSA's decade of experience and activities in professional integration would be seen as a whole by a much larger audience. Our hope is that this volume will become a reference document, encouraging the process of reintegration from the very beginning of the student's sojourn in the United States.

The book was prepared under the able direction of the book's coeditors, Mary Ann G. Hood, director of the English Language Institute at American University, and Kevin J. Schieffer, associate director of international and corporate programs at the School of Management of the State University of New York at Buffalo. In addition to the chapter authors, who contributed their accumulated expertise to the production of this book, a number of other people have made contributions that were essential to the success of the project. Special recognition for their guidance in the development of this book is extended to the members of the NAFSA/AID Steering Committee: William Fish, Arthur D. Little Management Educational Institute; Elena Garate, University of Southern California; John Van de Water, Oregon State University; and Willis Griffin, University of Kentucky. Jackie Seegers-Behrens, of Texas Tech University, also deserves recognition for her early efforts to adapt these principles into a reentry-transition course for foreign students at her institution. Finally, NAFSA/AID Program Director Robert Mashburn and his staff, Peter Schaub and others, have contributed extensively to making this publication a reality.

It is hoped that this publication will serve USAID participants and all students from the developing world as they prepare for their own professional reintegration into the important work of development.

Martin Limbird
Iowa State University
September 1983

The Authors

Patricia W. Barnes-McConnell is director of the Office of Women in International Development, Michigan State University

Harold Borko is director of the Graduate School of Library and Information Science, University of California-Los Angeles.

Stephen C. Dunnett is director of the Intensive English Language Institute, State University of New York at Buffalo.

Eileen Goldstein is a Ph.D. candidate in the Graduate School of Library and Information Science, University of California-Los Angeles.

Mary Ann G. Hood is director of the English Language Institute, American University.

D.Y. Lee is professor of civil engineering, Iowa State University.

Motoko Y. Lee is associate professor, Department of Sociology and Anthropology, Iowa State University.

Martin Limbird is director of the Office of International Educational Services, Iowa State University.

Michael J. Moravcsik is professor of physics, Institute of Theoretical Science, University of Oregon.

Mary Joy Pigozzi is director of the Non-Formal Education Information Center, College of Education, Michigan State University.

Kenneth A. Rogers is associate dean and director of international services, Indiana University.

Kevin J. Schieffer is associate director of international and corporate programs, School of Management, State University of New York at Buffalo.

Sally K. Williams is associate professor, Department of Home Economics Education, Iowa State University.

1.

Introduction

Kevin J. Schieffer

The most recent statistics on foreign students studying in the United States, as reported by the Institute of International Education, indicate that in 1981-82 there were 326,000 foreign students enrolled in U.S. colleges and universities. Of that figure approximately 75 percent, or 244,500, were from developing countries. These numbers represent the future business, government, and educational leaders of the developing world. Each individual represents the developing country's substantial commitment of resources to education as a foundation of its development efforts. What is particularly significant about the allocation of these resources, both human and financial, is the developing world's choice of the United States as a center for the education of its future leaders. That choice reflects credit on our postsecondary educational system, and is an indicator of the esteem in which our educational institutions are held overseas. It also represents a challenge to our educators to meet the needs and expectations of these individuals and their countries and thereby to assist in their development efforts.

Meeting that challenge has been the focus of a joint effort by the National Association for Foreign Student Affairs (NAFSA) and the U.S. Agency for International Development Office of International Training (OIT) for the past fifteen years. Much of this combined effort has focused on enriching the academic experience of students from the developing world, while also building a greater consciousness among international

Introduction

education professionals of these students' special needs. In the process OIT and NAFSA have addressed issues such as curricular relevancy, practical training, and cultural reentry. These efforts have contributed to the overall education of the student from the developing world. At the same time, each research project, seminar, and program has led to the recognition and acknowledgment that many problems remain unidentified and unsolved. Therefore, each year OIT and NAFSA have focused on building a body of knowledge about and a clearer understanding of the process of educating the student from the developing world in the United States.

In this book NAFSA and OIT address a long-standing problem for students from the developing world educated in the United States: the transition from academic training in the United States to a professional career in the home country. The process of professional integration, as it is identified here, expands on the cultural reentry concept to include the professional dimensions of reentry.

For any student, American or foreign, completing an academic education and entering the job market can be a traumatic and demoralizing experience. The worlds of student and professional are very different, each with its own set of rules, values, and behavioral patterns. Most colleges and universities offer a career guidance office that counsels and steers domestic students through this transition. In fact, most institutions now place greater emphasis on career guidance than ever before, due in part to the current economic environment and in part to the recognition that a student needs to be equipped with very different skills to function in the professional world.

For the foreign student, the passage from academic to professional is complicated by having to make the adjustment from a developed to a developing country. Colleges and universities in the United States are not generally equipped to deal with professional integration problems and are therefore unable to give meaningful guidance to the student returning to the developing world. Having returned home, the student from the developing world does not find institutions or services to help him in this transition process. Nor can the student generally look to parents or peers for guidance of this type. Parents and peers are likely to be confused themselves by the changes and transitional problems of the returned student.

All of these elements contribute to the student's sense of isolation in his own culture, precisely at the point when he must make a critical transition in his life. Absent are the university infrastructure with all of the academic and social amenities, the friends who knew and were sympathetic to the student's thoughts and emotions, and the freedom of being a student. This contributes to the problem and, in the end, to the success or failure of the professional integration of the returned student and his ability to contribute effectively to the long-term development of the home country.

This is not a new problem, but this book suggests some new solutions that focus on innovations and potential changes that could be made in our

Introduction

colleges and universities to address this problem. This book also suggests means for better informing the individual student of available resources and opportunities and of the problems inherent in the process of receiving an academic education in the United States and eventually returning home to a professional career. Some of the sections of this book are very specific about skills and knowledge acquisition; others define the transition process in terms of an educational continuum and thereby put the entire educational experience into perspective for the student. The overall objective is to supply the student with programmatic information that can be translated into a more relevant academic experience and a more successful and less traumatic transition into a professional career. Although the information contained in this book is geared specifically to the needs of developing world students, much of the information should be of interest and value to the international educator.

With the support and encouragement of the international educator, the developing country student will be able to integrate more effectively the information and direction provided by this book and thereby lessen the transitional problems the student will likely encounter upon return home. This publication may therefore be a useful tool for educators to use in the orientation of students, as well as the basis for periodic reorientation and predeparture programs. Many institutions that currently provide reentry or predeparture programs should find in this publication a valuable tool that carefully addresses some very basic but critical problems and needs of the developing world student in the reentry/professional integration process.

The student should review *Professional integration: A guide for students from the developing world* prior to departing from the home country for the United States. Each section addresses specific ways in which a student can seek direction and advice prior to departure and illustrates how an early assessment of one's academic plans from a broad perspective can facilitate an educational experience that is more relevant to the student and to the home country's needs and expectations.

Once the student has arrived in the United States he should periodically consult this book for information about the resources that can supplement the formal academic program and for advice on innovations that can make the general academic program more meaningful.

Upon return home, the student should consult this guide for advice on the professional transition process. The guide has meaningful suggestions for minimizing the sense of isolation through such activities as contacting other professionals trained in his field or who received training in the United States, planning and participating in continuing education programs, and participating in professional societies. This guide cannot solve all of the problems in the transition process, but it will give direction to the student, based on the cumulative experience of former students from the developing world who were educated in the United States and on the

Introduction

knowledge of international education professionals. This advice can minimize the sense of isolation and minimize the problems of professional integration.

Professional integration: A guide for students from the developing world will certainly not be the last attempt at addressing professional integration problems, nor does it address every issue and problem inherent in the process. It is, however, a tool for both students and educators that can be put to work in addressing the problems of transition from academic study in the U.S. to a professional career in a developing country. The book identifies the means for the student from the developing world to lend greater meaning to his education in the United States and thereby ensure a successful and dynamic transition into his role as a future leader of his home country.

2.
Alumni Networking

Kenneth A. Rogers

2.1. Introduction

Foreign alumni of U.S. colleges and universities, both individually and collectively, represent links with academic and nonacademic professional communities in the United States. The many who teach, conduct research, or have administrative positions in educational institutions abroad can serve as important channels of communication between their institutions and U.S. universities—especially the ones from which they have received their advanced academic or professional degrees. However, it appears that little is being done at present to further or facilitate two-way communication between foreign graduates of U.S. institutions and their former professors—now professional colleagues—in a systematic way. Neither the institutions involved nor their growing alumni constituencies in other countries have gone very far toward forging a network that is capable of serving the professional needs and interests of all concerned.

Yet, as several published studies have shown, U.S. institutions can contribute to the personal and professional development of their overseas alumni through various kinds of services or programs, many of which can be largely, if not totally, self-supporting. Practical approaches to foreign alumni programming are outlined in the booklet *Foreign alumni: Overseas links for U.S. institutions* (Goetzl and Stritter March 1980) and its predecessor, *The university and its foreign alumni: Maintaining overseas contact* (Forman and Moore 1964).

A common thrust of the most extensive and successful institutional programs currently operating is their inclusiveness. That is, they are more or less inclusive of all persons who have been associated with the university—not only students, but also former visiting scholars (lecturers, researchers, artists, etc.) who have been in residence on campus for a period of months or years, and even former short-term visitors who have addressed campus conferences and convocations or who have participated in other public events having educational significance. These "special alumni" receive from their U.S. host university, just as former students do, journals and special alumni publications, as well as invitations to overseas alumni conferences and other international alumni activities that take place either at the university or locally in other countries.

It follows that U.S. university alumni networks in developing countries should be as inclusive as possible. In other words, they should not be limited to graduates or other ex-students of a U.S. university if the overriding objective is to build productive working relationships among professionals with similar training-education and careers. The broader the base of network participation, the more effective and productive will be the exchange of ideas and information, the sharing of concerns, and the various kinds of professional collaboration that can be achieved through alumni networking.

For this reason, the term "alumni," as used in this chapter, refers to all individuals who have sojourned on U.S. campuses and who are now practicing professionals in the other countries. Particular attention will be given to the unique role they can play in providing foreign students with "strategic information and advice" (1) while the students are preparing for future professional careers through study at a U.S. university and (2) when they return to the home country to begin their life work. The final part of this chapter offers suggestions as to how returned graduates can assist in the process of building a network of U.S.-trained professionals by sharing their knowledge of and experience in U.S. higher education with compatriots who contemplate study in a U.S. graduate or professional school.

2.2. Making the Most of the U.S. Educational Experience

The alumni of a U.S. institution who are practicing professionals in a developing country represent sources of information and advice that can be enormously helpful to students from that country at the beginning of and throughout their study in that college or university. While the "strategic" value of the knowledge and experience these alumni can impart is perhaps greater for students who are pursuing a U.S. professional degree in engineering, business, or public administration, it is likely to be of considerable assistance as well to those who are preparing for a scholarly or scientific career of teaching or research in any university environment.

In recent years, NAFSA, the Council of Graduate Schools, the American Council on Education, and several national professional societies have promoted and focused considerable discussion among U.S. educators on the relevance of U.S. graduate programs to foreign students from developing countries. In a series of publications, beginning with the *A guide for the education of foreign students* (Benson and Kovach 1974), NAFSA has recommended approaches that might be put into effect within an institution (or an academic department) as part of a general strategy aimed at ensuring that the foreign students enrolled in graduate programs obtain the kind of educational experience that is most appropriate to (1) their previous scholastic preparation, (2) their present academic and postgraduate career objectives, and (3) the conditions under which they will be expected to practice their professions when they return to their respective home countries.

These discussions and studies have contributed to a growing awareness of two important points among university educators in the United States. First, foreign students admitted to U.S. institutions frequently encounter difficulties in their academic work that are, to a large extent, caused by inadequate communication between themselves and the Americans with whom they are associated in their academic pursuits. Second, foreign graduates of U.S. institutions are sometimes ill prepared (undertrained, overtrained, or poorly trained) for the careers they enter following their return to their home countries. Yet, unfortunately, it also remains true that, in most U.S. institutions, too little is being done in a systematic way to mitigate this situation. As a consequence, there is a continuing need to bring about more effective collegial communication—between the student and his academic adviser, between the student's sponsor and the academic departments of the U.S. host university, and others such as overseas alumni if the foreign student is to realize maximum benefit from his U.S. educational experience.

How can overseas alumni of U.S. universities be helpful? If consulted by the student at an early stage they can offer a number of practical recommendations (born of firsthand experience and knowledge gained while studying in a U.S. university) as well as current information on such matters as professional employment opportunities and trained manpower needs in the home country. This information can guide the student in selecting appropriate coursework, fields of concentration (specialization), topics for research, and practical training during his sojourn in the United States. Following are some specific suggestions as to how, with the help of alumni, the student can maximize the benefits he derives at different stages of his educational experience in the United States.

2.3. The U.S. Educational Experience

In conferring with an academic adviser on courses for the first term of enrollment, the student should take the occasion to review with the adviser his educational objectives and career goals. If, before leaving the home country, the student has had an opportunity to discuss these matters with any alumni of U.S. institutions, the information they provided should be shared with the academic adviser, particularly any information and advice as to the kinds of training that, in their experience or from their observations since returning home, are most appropriate for the present and future conditions.

The person or persons who have responsibility for advising the foreign student on academic matters are also responsible for reviewing his progress at regular intervals during the academic year and for advising him on adjustments in a program of study, the opportunities for gaining field experience, and other activities that might enrich the total educational experience (attendance at professional meetings, presentation of research papers, etc.). The persons responsible for advising the student on academic matters may, in cooperation with the designated campus Foreign Student Adviser (FSA) and the university's placement and career counseling office, assist him in obtaining practical training (work) experience in the United States prior to return to the home country.

The foregoing discussion is based on two assumptions: (1) that the FSA does not academically advise foreign students directly, except as academic advising enters other aspects of the advising responsibility, and (2) that the U.S. university has developed a workable system for the academic advising of *all* its students that assigns each student to a particular academic adviser in the appropriate department, division, or graduate school.

How these assignments are made or worked out is customarily left to the individual department or school concerned. At some institutions, a special effort is made to assign foreign students to academic advisers who have shown interest in or have had close association with foreign students over time. However, because it is sometimes difficult for an institution or department to select advisers who are especially knowledgeable about and sensitive to the particular needs of foreign students, there is a possibility that the student will be advised by someone who is unacquainted or only superficially acquainted with the critical human and economic issues that exist in the student's home country and that are perhaps uppermost in his thinking. This does not mean, however, that professors and faculty advisers are or will be indifferent to these concerns; if anything, it simply underscores the importance of informing the adviser of these concerns so that they can be taken into account in the advisement process.

Alumni Networking

In any case, the academic adviser will probably be the most important and influential person a student will encounter in the course of his stay in the United States, because the academic adviser may be the first person who becomes aware of the student's academic or personal problems. This is most often the case at a large university with a high enrollment of foreign students. Ideally, through open discussion with the student and close liaison with the FSA, the academic adviser will have an awareness of such matters as the student's culture and educational background and his present needs and future career objectives. Correspondence with the student's sponsor (if applicable) or with one or more interested alumni in his home country will also provide valuable background information to the adviser.

In the final analysis, however, the quality and relevance of the academic advising that the student obtains will depend to a large extent on his own approach to study in the United States. That is, the student must know what it is he wants to accomplish through pursuing a particular U.S. academic or professional degree, for, unless he has carefully defined his long-range objectives at the outset, he will not be in a position to clearly articulate basic needs and interests to those from whom he wishes to obtain advice.

Graduate foreign students should understand that there is considerable flexibility in course selection in most U.S. institutions; thus, while certain specific courses may be required in a given curriculum, generally, there are no totally prescribed programs. Academic advisers and professors will probably be most willing to help their students select appropriate electives—but it is up to the student to take the initiative in seeking their advice and assistance. This is the accepted U.S. practice at all levels of the university system, in contrast to the system the student may have known at home.

By rationalizing and relating his educational objectives to a specific career following return to the home country, the student greatly improves his chances of obtaining advice and information that will be truly useful to him as he endeavors to acquire essential knowledge and experience in a U.S. college or university that has been established primarily to serve the needs of American students. The U.S. institution's undergraduate and graduate curricula (courses, readings, research, etc.) are based primarily on (1) this country's economic, political, and social experience; (2) its agricultural practices and natural resources for industrial development; and (3) its unique cultural heritage and ethnic mix. As a result, the training offered may not be entirely applicable in the conditions extant in other countries.

Further, the predominant stress on theory and mathematical analysis—particularly in graduate programs—may come at the expense of an emphasis on problem identification and problem solving. This, in turn, can lead foreign graduate students to become engaged in research on highly theoretical problems rather than on problems that are directly applicable to conditions they will encounter as practitioners in their home countries. However, foreign graduate students should be cautioned against undertaking major research projects which focus on topics so particular to their home countries that the best reference tools and data sources are not available in the United States.

Obviously, the foregoing observations are quite general and cursory. They are meant both to amplify and to reinforce the initial suggestion that the student review his educational objectives and career goals with his academic adviser at an early date and that, if possible, he endeavor to draw upon the knowledge and experience of interested alumni in trying, with the help of his academic adviser, to relate his study program as much as possible to the environment in which he will practice as a professional. To this end, additional suggestions for and observations concerning alumni networking during the student's sojourn in the United States are offered in following sections.

2.3.1. The foreign student adviser

Institutes enrolling large numbers of foreign students usually employ one or more professional staff advisers who are assigned responsibility for handling the special problems that foreign students encounter in adjusting to the demands of living and studying in the United States. Known professionally as "Foreign Student Advisers" or "FSAs," these people can do much to assist the student in making the most of his experience at a U.S. university.

With the help of the university's foreign student adviser, the student should try to consult compatriots who are studying or teaching in other departments or schools on the campus. They can tell him about relevant course offerings, special resources, and facilities that are currently available (or that may become available) and would provide opportunities to enrich or enhance the student's learning experience in the United States. It is to the student's advantage to do this early on, for the sooner he discovers what is available—formally or informally, at his institution or through his institution from sources off campus—the better.

Generally, the FSA does not advise foreign students on the details of their academic programs, since such advice is properly given by the students' assigned academic or departmental advisers. The FSA is, nevertheless, an authoritative source of detailed information on many pertinent subjects, including home country employment and U.S. government regulations concerning practical training employment, among other things. The FSA is also prepared to explain or interpret institutional regulations and social customs and cultural patterns in the United States, as well as discuss knowledgeably many other matters of concern to foreign students.

In addition to carrying out these important advisory and information-disseminating functions, the FSA at many institutions plans and coordinates a variety of campus and community services for foreign students as part of an ongoing effort to ensure that they obtain optimum benefits from their stay in the United States. In this role, the FSA maintains liaison with national and international organizations, student-sponsoring agencies, and foreign government missions, as well as with interested campus and community groups, including foreign student nationality associations.

Regardless of whether there is an organization or association of students from a particular country on campus, the FSA can assist the student in contacting compatriots either before or soon after his arrival at the university. Early contact with fellow students or faculty who may be future professional colleagues has obvious immediate, as well as potential intermediate and long-term, advantages. Campus nationality associations, though primarily social in purpose, can not only further future alumni networking in the home country by fostering extracurricular interaction among students with common or parallel academic and career interests, but they can sometimes facilitate communication between member students and key individuals (including alumni) or professional groups in the home country. Assistance in identifying and contacting the latter can often be obtained from the FSA, members of the faculty with international interests, and the university's alumni office (see Section 2.4.1.).

Finally, the Foreign Student Adviser is frequently called upon by faculty colleagues to interpret foreign students' backgrounds, needs, and problems. Therefore, if the student is reluctant to approach his academic adviser or some other university official about some matter or personal concern, he should consult the FSA—without delay. (Experience at many institutions has shown that, very often, foreign students wait too long—until the matter has built up into a problem of major proportions—before seeking advice from the FSA. This can be a tragic mistake, and certainly it is unnecessary, as the FSA, like other faculty or administrators of the university, is keenly interested in the student's well-being. Above all, it should be understood that it is quite customary in the United States for students to ask their university advisers, peers, and others for advice about personal matters or concerns which, in other cultures, might be considered only "within the family.")

2.3.2. Keeping abreast of current developments at home

To the extent possible, students should try to stay abreast of current developments in the home country that relate to their future professional pursuits through reading newspapers or journals and by corresponding with former teachers, supervisors, or coworkers or with U.S. university alumni.

If the student cannot locate publications in the university library that provide current information on developments in his home country, he may, with the help of a librarian, find them in a library elsewhere on campus. Failing this, the student might contact the education-cultural counselor or attaché of his country's embassy in Washington to request that he be sent appropriate information materials on a regular basis during his stay in the United States.

The information obtained from these various sources, or perhaps from major newspapers and journals published in the United States, can guide the student in planning his program of study and in making appropriate mid-course adjustments to take into account changed or changing conditions or needs in the home country. Additional useful guidance can sometimes be obtained from a campus career planning or counseling office, a school or university placement office, or a home country employment service.

2.3.3. Professional associations

To the extent possible, the student should acquaint himself with and participate in the activities of the leading U.S. professional association(s) in the appropriate field—and their international sections, where applicable.

The academic adviser can suggest when, how, and what kind of involvement in professional association activities would be most beneficial while the student is the the United States as well as after he has returned home. Through participation in the activities of professional societies in the United States, the student may be able to make contact with future professional colleagues from his home country who, upon their return, are likely to be participants in and beneficiaries of an active alumni network of professionals with similar training, education, and careers. The importance of involving oneself in such activities is discussed in Chapter 3, *"The scientist or scholar interacts: Communication and interpersonal relations in the developing countries."*

2.4. Preparing for Return to the Home Country

In consultation with faculty of the school or department, the Foreign Student Adviser, the staff of the university's alumni office, or others, the student should identify professionals in his field at home who can facilitate the process of getting "reincorporated" or established successfully in a career following the return home.

Alumni Networking

As indicated in the introduction to this chapter, few U.S. institutions have, to date, encouraged foreign alumni networking through special programming or services designed to facilitate communication among faculty, students on the U.S. campus, and alumni in other countries. Because of this, the student may encounter some difficulties in his effort to identify and locate alumni in the home country who are professionals in his field, and who might be both willing and able to provide appropriate information and advice on various matters of concern as he prepares to return home. "Matters of concern" in this context refers to whatever apprehensions or uncertainties the student may have at this stage with regard to becoming reincorporated (professionally or socially) or established in the career for which he has been preparing.

One typical difficulty in many institutions is finding current addresses for and up-to-date information on the professional pursuits of alumni in the home country who have been identified as potential sources of advice and to whom the student might write some months in advance of his planned return. In some cases, the files of the academic department or school will contain the current addresses and professional biodata of such alumni. Otherwise, it is possible that this information is available from the Foreign Student Adviser's office or the university's alumni office.

If, however, the current addresses and biodata of alumni with whom the student may wish to correspond cannot be located in university files, he should consider trying to obtain this information through the binational commission, the Cultural Affairs Officer of the U.S. Embassy (USIS), or the USAID mission in the home country. Binational commissions in many countries maintain updated addresses of former Fulbright or other U.S. government grantees (including former AID participants). Of course, if the U.S. university has an alumni club or if an association of American university alumni exists in the home country, it may be possible to secure the needed information by writing to the appropriate association officer(s). It is advisable that the student explain, in a letter requesting current addresses and biodata of alumni, that he wishes to contact them for advice and information prior to his planned return to the home country. If the student is willing to play a similar advisory role for future students from his home country, this should be indicated in the letter to the binational commission or alumni association, giving an address in the home country for their future reference.

Once the student has the necessary addresses and biodata, and as soon as plans for returning home are reasonably certain, he should send inquiries to alumni. This will enable alumni to respond in a more helpful and prompt fashion. In addition to discussing salient aspects of his U.S. study and practical training experience, as well as career aspirations or concerns, the student may wish to enclose a personal resume or curriculum vitae that has been prepared in accordance with standard (U.S. or home country) professional practices or specifications of the university placement office. Copies of articles the student has authored while in the United States might also be enclosed or sent under separate cover, particularly if cited in the letter or resume. Finally, alumni should be given a home country address that they can use to write to the student after he has returned home.

While there is no guarantee that this initiative on the student's part will bring either a prompt or a fully satisfying response, it is well justified by the adage "nothing ventured, nothing gained." Even a perfunctory response or no response at all can be regarded as something of a gain—especially if it tends to corroborate other evidence that there is a low level (or total absence) of alumni networking in the home country, which is a situation that the student will need to take into account in preparing for return.

2.4.1. The university alumni office

Before departing for home, the student should leave a current home country mailing address with the U.S. university's alumni office or foreign student office as well as with appropriate persons (deans, department chairman, or faculty) in the school or department.

According to a 1977 NAFSA survey of 100 institutions enrolling more than 1,000 foreign students, postgraduation contact with foreign alumni has been largely handled through university alumni offices, with only occasional contact being carried out through academic departments (Goetzl and Stritter 1980). The survey findings further indicate that "relatively little is being done to obtain names and addresses of foreign alumni residing abroad" and that the great majority of U.S. institutions do not publish a directory of foreign alumni.

In contrast to this rather dismal picture of institutional recordkeeping, the survey suggests (and the author's own investigations have confirmed) that there are still many ways in which universities maintain contact with their foreign alumni. Quite a few universities are, in fact, assisting in the formation of alumni associations abroad and, in addition, are sending alumni publications to their overseas constituents. But to do these things economically, it is essential that they have current addresses and up-to-date biodata on file.

Thus, foreign alumni should see to it that their names, current addresses, and other data are correctly recorded in files maintained by the university's alumni office or those kept by the foreign student office or the school or department in which they were enrolled. Students especially interested in receiving alumni publications or in initiating or participating in alumni activities in the home country should make this known to the school or department, the FSA, and the alumni office before they leave.

2.4.2. Helping the admissions office

The returning student who expects to be in a position to volunteer some time to discuss study at a U.S. university with prospective applicants for admission who seek training in the same field should make this known to the Foreign Student Adviser or departmental admissions director before departure for home, so that he can be provided with up-to-date material and information on such matters as current requirements and procedures.

At present, relatively few universities regularly enlist the services of their alumni abroad in screening or orientation of prospective students, although there are indications that this practice will become more widespread in the future. There also seems to be an increasing interest among campus placement services to provide guidance and maintain some contact with students returning to their home countries after they have completed programs of study in U.S. universities.

These activities, among others that will be mentioned later in this chapter, are or can become the foundation for home country alumni networking, for they provide not only valuable public services, but also personally rewarding experiences and recognition for the alumni involved.

2.5. Returning to the Home Country

A foreign student need not be completely "on his own" in making reentry to the home country environment and in making the subsequent transition to a professional position. As indicated, there are probably persons on the scene—fellow alumni—who can facilitate the process of becoming reincorporated or established in a professional career. They can, if nothing else, provide the returned student the kind of moral support or encouragement that is needed to overcome "reverse culture shock" or any of the tensions and anxieties that are commonly experienced by individuals after returning from extended sojourns abroad. Alumni networking, while not indispensable for a smooth reentry or for professional integration, can nevertheless enhance and accelerate these processes. It also represents a means of following up on one's U.S. study experience in ways that can further professional development and help provide other benefits as well. Some of the benefits of alumni networking will be noted throughout the following discussion.

2.5.1. Alumni activities in the home country

Soon after returning home, the newly trained professional may wish to consult other professionals in the field who share a common background of study in the United States and who might be in a position to assist in one

Alumni Networking

way or another. To locate or contact such persons the returned student may call on either the local (home country) association of his U.S. university or a local chapter of his U.S. university's alumni association (if one or both exist) for assistance. Otherwise, an official agency, such as the binational commission, a USIS information center, or the USAID mission, may be able to help arrange contact with U.S.-trained professionals in a particular field or perhaps with organizations whose members include such persons.

Returned students might consider offering informal talks or lectures on study in the United States at local secondary or postsecondary institutions or serving as alumni advisers to persons in the locality who contemplate study toward a U.S. professional degree in the same field; this assumes, of course, that there is interest expressed in response to such overtures and that the individual's time will allow for such "public service" activities. Generally, activities of this kind are most effective when carried out through a local alumni association or under the auspices of the binational commission, a USIS information center, or the field office of a cooperating private (nongovernmental) educational service agency such as the Institute of International Education (IIE), the African-American Institute (AAI), America-Mideast Educational and Training Services (AMIDEAST), the Fulbright Program, the Latin American Scholarship Program of American Universities (LASPAU), or the Rotary International Foundation. These activities can also help alumni gain some public recognition, while winning the respect and appreciation of persons in their community.

Following are some basic guidelines for providing information and advice to prospective students of U.S. universities:

1. Published information for prospective students should be as up-to-date, accurate, and complete as possible.*
2. Particular emphasis should be placed on the importance of selecting an appropriate U.S. institution with attention to the quality, content, and suitability of the educational programs offered; the facilities available; and the qualifications of faculty in relation to the prospective student's academic preparation and professional career interests and goals.
3. Prospective students should be encouraged to consult a student counselor or other qualified staff members of the binational commission or USIS information center for further assistance.
4. Prospective students should be encouraged to solicit, from both alumni and currently enrolled students of the institutions they are considering, suggestions, evaluative comments, and insights concerning each institution's strengths and weaknesses.

---

*Prospective students can be referred to the binational commission, USIS libraries, or other reliable sources if current literature is not available.

5. After acceptance by a U.S. institution, the prospective student should be encouraged to ask a local alumnus to write a letter to the student's major department in that institution; such a letter might describe the student's primary interest and objectives in seeking professional training in the United States, as well as his special needs or requirements in terms of supplementary coursework, practical experience, or both.

Alumni enthusiasm about their own U.S. institution will no doubt favorably impress the students they are advising. Prospective students will be even more favorably impressed, however, if they are made aware of the existence of an alumni network in their own country that not only can contribute to the professional integration of returning graduates, but can also continue to further their careers in various ways.

It is to be hoped, that having returned home, the foreign student will have become the beneficiary of the home country alumni network and can testify to its capacity to further professional integration by facilitating contact among individuals with similar professional training and interests. Perhaps, too, the returned student will have discovered other benefits of alumni networking, such as providing a channel of communication through which one learns of opportunities for linkages between local institutions, agencies, or firms and counterparts in the United States or some other country. Academic linkages involving the exchange of scholars, joint research, or other cooperative activities have become a major aspect of international educational interchange in recent years and, from all indications, they will become even more vital in the years ahead.

Often, linkages serve a combination of the following purposes: (1) personal and professional development; (2) institutional development in teaching, research, and public service; and (3) regional, national, and international development in the fields of education, agriculture, manufacturing, trade, and the administration of health care systems, social welfare, housing, telecommunications, and so forth. While it is not necessary that the institutions or individuals involved in a particular linkage program have identical or even shared objectives, it is essential that the program provide an acceptable measure of reciprocal benefits over time.

Universities in the United States are becoming increasingly aware that interinstitutional linkages can be promoted, nurtured, and sustained through special alumni programs designed to further the professional advancement of individuals at different stages of their careers in their home countries.

It is perhaps important to note, in this connection, that the continuing expansion of higher education in most developing countries offers abundant opportunities for linkages with institutions (or college and university consortia) in the United States. Among the most promising areas for

Alumni Networking

cooperation are (1) the training of university faculty and administrators; (2) institutional research, administration, and organization; (3) curriculum development and related activites, including English-as-a-second-language and American studies programs. Cooperation is the key word, for what is sought (and what is most likely to satisfy current as well as long-term future institutional needs) are genuine partnerships with U.S. universities based on mutual respect, shared interests, and reciprocal benefits. And while there are now (and will, for the foreseeable future, continue to be) opportunities for cooperation in virtually all academic disciplines and professional fields, the ones that seem preeminent are education (teacher training, instructional systems technology, etc.), business and public administration, and applied sciences (computer science, engineering).

Professionals working in the field of higher education may, from time to time, need to locate U.S. or U.S.-trained specialists or resource persons for planning and program development purposes in their institutions or agencies. Here, again, an alumni network may provide a valuable "resource locator" service. Or, alternatively, professionals may wish to plug into an existing U.S. system or network, such as the Register for International Service in Education (RISE), a computer-based referral service administered by the Institute of International Education. RISE enables universities, professional-technical institutes, research centers, and government ministries outside the United States to locate qualified educators, specialists, researchers, and consultants for both short- and long-term overseas assignments. Its purpose is to match the needs of educational institutions, agencies, and development projects in other countries with the qualifications of U.S. experts in virtually all fields of higher education.*

Finally, when foreign alumni have occasion to revisit the United States they should try to include a visit to their U.S. university so as to discuss with former professors, the FSA, and alumni office staff their professional pursuits, involvement in alumni activities, and retrospective views on their U.S. study experience. The FSA might also be able to arrange for foreign alumni to meet with fellow countrymen who are currently studying at the university.

2.5.2. Continuing education and professional development for alumni

"Alumni colleges" or other educational programs designed especially for alumni are not a new development on the U.S. college-university scene. Indeed, these programs have grown and become quite widespread and highly diversified. Some are also offered off campus at various locations in

---

*Further particulars on RISE may be obtained from IIE, 809 United Nations Plaza, New York, NY 10017.

the United States or, occasionally, overseas. However, few institutions have yet mounted a full-fledged continuing education program specifically directed at the needs of their foreign alumni abroad. Such programs are, nevertheless, considered both feasible and desirable by continuing education and university extenstion authorities whose institutions have had experience in providing courses of instruction for U.S. nationals in other countries (Armed Forces personnel, employees of U.S. and multinational firms, etc.) in a variety of professional fields. In some cases, regular faculty of the university offering the programs are often deployed to overseas locations to teach the courses or conduct advanced-level seminars, especially where the courses involve credit toward a U.S. degree.

It seems likely, therefore, that, in time, there will be opportunities for foreign alumni of U.S. institutions (and others) to enroll in continuing education courses or to participate in other U.S. university-sponsored professional development programs conducted in their home countries by U.S. faculty, perhaps in collaboration with professional colleagues on the scene. As this is being written, one large midwestern university is in the process of launching an international alumni outreach program that is aimed explicitly at (1) facilitating foreign alumni leadership development; (2) improving communication between the university and its overseas constituents; and (3) encouraging faculty-student-alumni involvement in various cooperative projects, including special conferences, seminars, and short-term "continuing education" courses taught by teams of its faculty "on location" in other countries. Some of the faculty who will be engaged to teach courses, lead seminars, or conduct workshops for alumni are persons who are traveling abroad to attend conferences or are working temporarily in another country as consultants under the auspices of AID or an international technical assistance agency. It is expected that the courses, seminars, and workshops offered through the university's international alumni outreach program will be of particular interest and benefit to "senior" foreign alumni who received their U.S. training some years ago and who wish to take "refresher courses" on developments of professional interest to them, acquire new knowledge or skills in management, or work with computers and other new technology.

Foreign alumni may wish to consider initiating activities of this kind through the local alumni association, if one exists. For example, it might be possible to take advantage of the future visits of American specialists or scholars and arrrange for them to meet with alumni, give lectures, or lead discussions on topics of professional interest.

Locally arranged programs that tap the expertise of itinerant U.S. faculty or specialists in nonacademic professions can be undertaken informally and at minimum expense either to alumni hosts or to the American visitors. Programs of this type could, in turn, lead to the establishment of ongoing linkages involving exchanges, joint research, or other cooperative

Alumni Networking

activities with reciprocal professional and institutional benefits for home country and U.S. participants alike. In some countries, limited amounts of U.S. linkage "seed money" funding might be obtained from a local American chamber of commerce or business group (i.e., Rotary Club) from the binational commission, or through the offices of the cultural affairs officer (USIS) of the U.S. embassy. To locate American business groups or firms operating in a country that might be interested, as a public service, in supporting educational or professional development and training programs sponsored by local U.S. university alumni, alumni should contact the commercial attaché of the nearest U.S. embassy or consulate for advice and assistance.

There are promising possibilities for programming designed to "follow up" on a U.S. study experience. However, in the absence of in-country programming provided by a U.S. university through an international alumni outreach effort, it will probably be necessary for interested alumni to take the initiative in setting up a program to accomplish the same thing using all means available, including the alumni, the binational commission, private business groups or individual firms, and others. The main difficulty in this endeavor will be receiving early notice of the forthcoming visits of the American scholars or specialists who might participate as consultants, resource persons, lecturers, or trainers in such programs. The more lead time the program planners have for contacting and corresponding with prospective American visitors, the greater the chances of being able to work out the program details (dates, the honorarium to be offered, topics to be covered, materials to be used, any necessary registration charges, etc.) and make arrangements for transportation, lodging, equipment, and facilities.

If alumni have not had experience in planning or administering programs of this kind, it may be helpful to consult others in the community who have, or, again, to seek advice from the local binational commission, USIS, or USAID staff. Mistakes at the outset or miscalculations at any stage in the development and presentation of the programming first attempted should by no means discourage anyone from trying again for, indeed, "trial and error" is the only approach that can be followed in these circumstances, especially when pioneering in a new area. Whatever the mistakes or miscalculations, the chances are good that a first effort will be rewarded with success, and that subsequent efforts will be not only more "trouble free," but also even more successful—partly because the alumni planners will have demonstrated the actual and potential value of continuing education and professional development programs initiated by and for the benefit of U.S. university alumni and their compatriot professional colleagues.

While it is perhaps too soon to declare the advent of a new era of international alumni follow-up initiatives and programming in developing countries, there is good reason to anticipate that activity of this kind will become more significant and widespread in the near future, particularly as home country alumni networking increases and U.S. institutions initiate, improve, and extend their programs and services for foreign alumni in the years ahead. By communicating an interest in or desire for continuing education and professional development programming to his U.S. university, the returned student may help accelerate progress toward programming of the type discussed. If, in doing so, an individual can speak for fellow U.S.-trained professionals as well as for himself, the chances for a positive, definitive response are, of course, considerably better than if he were speaking only as an individual. In other words, U.S. institutions are likely to be most responsive when they become aware of a "critical mass" of potential participants in educational activities of this kind, which necessarily entail additional or extraordinary expense of limited institutional resources such as programming funds, staff, and faculty. The larger the potential audiences for overseas continuing education and professional development offerings, the more economical they become for the U.S. institutions administering them.

Cost sharing will, in any case, be the most feasible means of financing pilot programs. As the demand for these programs increases, they should become practically or entirely self-supporting and independent of limited institutional budgetary resources. Through ingenuity, resourcefulness, and initiatives on the part of interested alumni in the countries in which follow-up programming is being or will be provided, funds may be raised locally (from home country or U.S. government or private business sources) for subsidies to help keep the costs to individual participants as low as possible. Ways to locate possible sources of contributions in the home country have been suggested earlier in this section with reference to alumni-initiated local programs utilizing visiting Americans as resource persons.

2.6. Conclusion

Alumni networking can assist an individual before, during, and after his study at a U.S. university, but, most especially, it can assist in facilitating professional integration following return to the home country. A worldwide network of alumni of U.S. institutions has tremendous potential for furthering international educational interchange while benefiting individual professionals throughout their careers, as well as the establishments in which they work. The immediate challenge is to activate the network in each country and to mobilize through it the enormous resources it encompasses for the advancement of national and international development.

The network is there—available to returned students if they wish to draw upon it. The initiative to activate it, however, must be taken by alumni themselves.

References Cited

Benson, August, and Joseph Kovach, eds. 1974. *A guide for the education of foreign students—Human resources development.* Washington, D.C.: NAFSA.

Forman, Robert E., and Forrest G. Moore. 1964. *The university and its foreign alumni: Maintaining overseas contact.* Minneapolis: University of Minnesota Press.

Goetzl, Sylvia, and Jill Stritter, eds. 1980. *Foreign alumni: Overseas links for U.S. institutions, a report on an AID/NAFSA survey in 1977.* Washington, D.C.: NAFSA.

Bibliography

Baron, Marvin. 1979. *The relevance of U.S. graduate programs to foreign students from developing countries.* Washington, D.C.: National Association for Foreign Student Affairs.

Council for Advancement and Support of Education. 1974. *A manual of international alumni relations.* Washington, D.C.: Council for Advancement and Support of Education.

Duge, Edna. 1963. International alumni groups. *Overseas* (December): 9-11.

Dunnett, Stephen C. 1982. *Management skills training for foreign engineering students—An assessment of need and availability.* Washington, D.C.: National Association for Foreign Student Affairs.

Eide, Ingrid, ed. 1970. *Students as links between cultures.* Paris: UNESCO.

Flack, Michael J., and Seth Spaulding, eds. 1976. *The world's students in the United States.* New York: Praeger Publishers.

Heyduk, Daniel, ed. 1979. *Education and work: A symposium, 1978.* New York: Institute of International Education.

Hood, Mary Ann G., and Kathleen Reardon-Anderson. 1979. *235,000 foreign students in U.S. colleges and universities—Impact and response.* Washington, D.C.: National Association for Foreign Student Affairs.

Jenkins, Hugh M., rapporteur. 1980. *The relevance of U.S. education to students from developing countries—A report of the fourth AID/NAFSA workshop.* Washington, D.C.: National Association for Foreign Student Affairs.

Johnson, Dixon C. 1970. Asian alumni look back on their American experiences. *International Educational and Cultural Exchange.* (Summer): 77-82.

Kimmel, P., W. Lybrand, and W. Ockey. 1969. *Participant assessment of A.I.D. training programs. First Annual Report.* Washington, D.C.: Agency for International Development/Office of International Training.

LASPAU. 1977. *LASPAU Alumni Survey.* Cambridge, Mass.: Latin American Scholarship Program of American Universities.

Lee, Motoko. 1981. *Needs of foreign students from developing countries at U.S. colleges and universities.* Washington, D.C.: National Association for Foreign Student Affairs.

Rogers, Kenneth A., et al. 1976. *Overseas counselor's manual.* New York: College Entrance Examination Board.

Schuiteman, Robert, and Barbara Ostrander, eds. 1972. *An inquiry into departmental policies and practices in relation to the graduate education of foreign students.* Washington, D.C.: National Association for Foreign Student Affairs.

Wichlac, Jerry. 1974. Thirty-seven program ideas for foreign alumni. *Techniques,* October. Washington, D.C.: American Alumni Council.

Wulf, Jerry Ernst. 1978. USC Foreign Alumni Association. *Exchange,* Spring.

3.
The Scientist or Scholar Interacts: Communication and Interpersonal Relations in the Developing Countries

Michael J. Moravcsik

3.1. Introduction and Outline

The intellectual professions are generally marked by being highly collective, interactive, and universal. This is particularly true for professionals in the natural sciences (henceforth referred to simply as scientists), where the cumulativeness and objectivity of the subject matter contribute especially strongly toward such collectivity and interactiveness (Moravcsik 1980). Indeed, it would be practically impossible for somebody in the natural sciences to carry on a productive career on a desert island, cut off from the rest of the world, even if he were supplied with the best scientific instruments and given the supplies and auxiliary facilities needed for scientific work. A study of the scientific community reveals immediately the elaborate and highly effective worldwide network of communication that operates among scientists, cutting across national, political, religious, ideological, social, ethnic, and chronological differences. This is so true that many of the most frequently used measures of scientific activity utilize the communication system, relying on the number of publishing authors, the number of publications, and the number of citations.

In the social sciences, the degree of universality is less marked than it is in the natural sciences, as it is in the humanities. In these fields, a greater variety of different methods, points of view, ideologies, and interests can co-exist side by side, and the subject matter to be studied also varies much more from country to country. Yet, even in these fields, certain worldwide

The Scientist or Scholar

trends, ideas, and methods are in evidence, and researchers in a given subfield and with a particular focus of interest are distributed widely the world over. Books, journals, and lectures signify the need of these researchers to interact and to rely on each other in their scholarly endeavors.

Interaction and communication, therefore, are among the most essential tools of scientific or scholarly work. At the same time, they are among the most pervasive deficiencies in the surroundings of a scientist or scholar in a developing country. Indeed, isolation can be named as the foremost obstacle to the evolution of science and scholarship in the Third World (Salam 1966). Countless testimonials from scientists and scholars in the developing countries attest to the validity of this statement.

It is, therefore, the purpose of this chapter to discuss this isolation in detail, to analyze the ways in which this isolation manifests itself, and then to suggest ways in which this isolation can be lessened or eliminated. Some of the "countermeasures" must be undertaken while the student from the developing country is still receiving his advanced education in the United States, while others must await his return to his home country. Some of these measures require new financial resources, but many can be undertaken using existing latent resources and opportunities. Some can be organized by the scientist or scholar of the developing country himself, while others need to be put in place by the worldwide scientific and scholarly community. Even in the latter case, however, action is unlikely to occur unless there is intensive campaigning for such measures by scientists and scholars from the developing countries themselves. Hence, in the final analysis, a student returning to this home from advanced education abroad should be familiar with all these problems and with the suggested remedial actions, and he should also be prepared to initiate new programs and action.

The next section (marked 3.2) discusses the various objectives and functions of communication for scientists and scholars. This is followed, in section 3.3 by an analysis of the dual aspect of linkages in local and international contexts. Section 3.4 explains the various mechanisms for interaction among scientists and among scholars. The next part, section 3.5, is the main focal point of the whole chapter, since it deals with remedies for the problems described in other sections. As mentioned earlier, both the period of education abroad and the time after return home are included in the discussion of suggested actions.

3.2. The Objectives of Communication

From the point of view of the scientist or scholar and from the point of view of the developing country where he is located, communication and interaction have a multitude of different objectives and functions. Communication is an activity that takes place in a multidimensional world of science and scholarship, and, hence, the aims of this activity are also multidimensional. These dimensions are very different from each other, and connect the scientist or scholar with groups of people of great variety. That there are thus many different justifications for communication does not weaken, but rather strengthens, the importance of communication. Different people may be personally interested in different dimensions, but all of them would find reasons for considering communication an indispensable aspect of scientific or scholarly work.

3.2.1. To provide information

Perhaps the most immediate function of communication is the transmittal of information. In communicating, the scientist or scholar sends and receives information. This information can be of various types. In the simplest case, this information is a piece of "fact." For example, the scientist may need the value of a parameter that goes into his calculation of some other predicted effect, or, the historian, studying the interplay of influences in an important event, may require some biographical information on one of the key individuals in the event. Such information can be obtained from a book or from another individual who knows it.

Information can, however, also be of a more subtle kind. News about some important new developments in the field; about new research directions just opened up; about a meeting, discussion, or debate concerning a controversial question; about a comparison of alternative ways of reaching a research target; and about the constantly rearranging patterns of scientific personnel and their locations are all among the pieces of information that contribute to the foundation on which a scientist or scholar must build his own work.

It is essential to stress that, from the point of view of the country where the scientist or scholar resides, his function as a channel of information into the country far exceeds in importance his contributions through personal research. To take the example of the sciences, in developing countries, the research done by the nationals of a given country represents perhaps one-thousandth of the total new scientific research produced around the world. Thus, an overwhelming proportion of the scientific results needed by that country for its technological development work, for its general education, and for its decision-making process must come from abroad. In fact, in this respect, the scientifically advanced countries are in a different position only quantitatively; for example, about two-thirds of the science produced in the world comes from outside the United States. All countries are net importers of scientific knowledge, but in a developing country, this "balance of trade" is simply more extreme. From this point of view, therefore, the scientific research of somebody in a developing country can simply be

The Scientist or Scholar

regarded as overhead, a price to be paid for that person's capacity to serve as a channel of scientific information into the country. Only those actively engaged in scientific and scholarly work are in the position of seeking out, receiving, sifting, interpreting, and evaluating the worldwide flow of information and transmitting it to those in the country who would utilize it for its various purposes.

This realization has three operational consequences. First, strong concern with exactly what the personal research field of a scientist is does not appear to be warranted, since the scientist's area of expertise and information-gathering ability is much broader than his particular research problem. Second, the education of a scientist, particularly in a developing country, must be very broad, so that he can serve as a channel of information in a large area of science. Third, once this scientist has returned home after education abroad, mechanisms should be found for him to actually serve as a transmitter of information, outside his duties in connection with personal research work. Since it is highly unlikely that the science administrators of his country will be aware of this responsibility, the scientist himself must bear the burden of creating such channels.

3.2.2. To be stimulated by ideas

Since scientific or scholarly activity is highly interactive, every researcher is likely to be stimulated by knowledge of the ideas of other researchers in the field. In some cases, the stimulation may come from hearing about an important breakthrough created by one of the leading minds. This breakthrough then can be elaborated on, tested, applied, and adapted to particular local circumstances. Stimulated by the ideas of others, scientists and scholars are also moved to produce better ideas, to explore new ways of thinking about problems, and to learn from the weaknesses and limitations of the ideas of others. It is said that the great American inventor Sperry delighted in hearing about failures in the ideas and attempts of others because that information steered his own mind toward ways in which the attempt that failed could be turned into success by a different approach. Just as a community becomes inbred and stagnant in the absence of intermarriage with outsiders, the brain of a scientist also becomes inbred and sterile if it is restricted to the examination of only its own products.

3.2.3. To provide opportunities for critique

It was mentioned earlier that science is an objective undertaking, meaning that there is a method within the scientific community to decide who is right and who is wrong, and that there is a common perception within this community about the nature of the subject under investigation.

Part of this method is the ongoing dialogue among scientists concerning new phenomena discovered and new explanations given for these phenomena. Often this dialogue takes the form of an adversary encounter in which a proponent of an idea defends it and some colleagues try to find its inadequacies. Similarly, a newly performed experiment with some novel results would be scrutinized by some other scientists to ascertain that the experiment was performed in an appropriate way.

In the world of scholars, such objectivity may not exist, and many different approaches and ideas may exist side by side, but this only enhances the opportunity for debate and critique. In this case, the power of a new idea may be established not by its agreement with some objective reality, but, instead, by its ability to influence the thinking and work of many other scholars in the field. This influence is tested through dialogue, debate, and critique.

In either realm, the importance of new research depends on its transmission to and acceptance by the scientific and scholarly community or the technologists and others who use the ideas for practical purposes. An idea in the head of its creator, unless communicated and accepted, has no value because it dies with the death of its creator, having pleased no one else.

The lack of opportunities for communication in the developing countries has often meant that scientists and scholars spend valuable talent, resources, and time in research directions that are false, sterile, and uninteresting to anyone else. Needless to say, such research will not contribute to any of the social aims of scientific or scholarly activity. It will not be of practical use, it will not influence the world view of the people, it will not contribute to the prestige of the country, and it will not represent a realization of the aspiration to become excellent, to become a leader, and to make strides toward exploring the unknown. Such a sterile and inbred research situation can be prevented if fellow scientists and scholars in the country and outside it critique the activities of researchers.

3.2.4. To have research collaboration

Especially in the natural sciences, but also increasingly in the social sciences and, to a much lesser extent, in the humanities, research collaborations have become frequent. The extreme form of collaboration manifests itself in "big science" fields, such as high energy physics, space-based observational astronomy, and some aspects of geophysics, in which the number of authors for a single scientific paper might well exceed 100. But even in areas of "little science," publications with two or three authors are very common. Often the two authors are located in the same institution, but this is not always so; research collaboration may thus involve communication over a distance, or travel by at least one author for the duration of the research.

The Scientist or Scholar

Such research cooperation can be particularly advantageous for someone in a developing country where the number of researchers in a given field is very low and where research facilities are scarce and often not well equipped. If such a scientist or scholar can establish a collaborative research relationship with a colleague of similar interests who is located in a more advanced country, the resulting cooperation can be beneficial for all those involved. In some cases, such research collaboration involves scientists or scholars from other developing countries in the region. In fact, there are various international agencies such as the Organization of American States, UNESCO, or ASEAN that specifically encourage such collaborative research by establishing communication networks within a given geographical region.

3.2.5. To receive recognition

Scientists and scholars, like most other people, are motivated toward their work by a large number of different factors. Perhaps the most important motivations are internal; that is, they stem from the feeling of curiosity, fascination, and esthetic satisfaction involved in the pursuit of scientific or scholarly work. Internal motivation is particularly important in a developing country, where the external obstacles in the path of such work are much larger, and where sometimes the society may be noncomprehending, insensitive, and indifferent toward such work.

Yet it is hard, even for the strongest personalities, to survive on internal motivation alone. Outside recognition, therefore, is important in generating high morale and in giving strength in the face of adverse circumstances. Outside recognition from the scientific or scholarly community is particularly valuable in this respect since it comes from a group of knowledgeable peers.

But such recognition, especially if it comes from abroad, can also mean much in dealing with those in the country who administer scientific and scholarly activities. The saying that "nobody is a prophet in his own country" is singularly applicable to scientists and scholars in developing countries. They often have little credibility in the eyes of their compatriots, who are not in a position to assess the quality of local scientists and who, therefore, tend to assign low esteem to all of them, except to those who are skillful in projecting a favorable image of themselves. In such a situation of uncertain criteria, recognition from abroad, especially if originating from sources whose credentials are especially strong, can establish the deserved standing of a scientist or scholar in his own country.

To be able to attract such recognition, however, the scientist or scholar must not only be proficient in his own field, but also have contacts in the worldwide scientific or scholarly community. In principle, such recognition can be acquired on the strength of written publications alone, but, in most cases, personal acquaintance is an important factor, since such acquaintance provides much more information about the scientist or scholar than merely his published papers.

3.2.6. To ensure logistic cooperation

Neither a scholar nor a scientist can carry out his work without the logistic cooperation of a large number of individuals. For example, to carry out any project, a scientist needs scientific instruments; supplies and repair facilities; an institution to work in; a building to be housed in; research funds to pay for various expenses of scientific work; someone to type the research publication, prepare figures, and duplicate copies; a journal editor to receive the research paper, send it to referees, and accept it for publication; and colleagues in technology, in public education, and in scientific organization and administration to whom the research results are transmitted. In research involving big science, the scientist also needs to gain the support of fellow scientists who allocate space and time in the large research facilities.

Therefore, articulateness, skill in interpersonal relations, tact in dealing with a variety of different people, diplomacy in interacting with administrators, and persuasive ability when presenting a case before scientific colleagues are very important assets to a scientist and, perhaps to a slightly lesser extent, to a scholar.

3.2.7. To transmit the results of scientific and scholarly research

As mentioned earlier, the scientist depends on transmitting the results of his research to other scientists or to people outside science who will use them, and the same holds true for scholars. Thus, one of the very central aspects and objectives of communication is the transmittal of research results. The most traditional means of transmission is publication in books, journal articles, or reports. Therefore, the scientist or scholar must know how to write clearly, convincingly, interestingly, and concisely. Furthermore, especially if he is from a small country with a language not among the common world languages, a scientist or scholar needs good writing skills not only in his native language, but also in one of those languages that are used for communication in the international scientific and scholarly community.

Such writing skills are often not emphasized during the person's education in local schools, and they are practically never stressed when the student goes abroad for advanced education. In this respect, the social sciences and the humanities are in a somewhat better position than the natural sciences, but in no case is the situation satisfactory. In addition, certain cultural heritages discourage an extroverted, articulate, highly communicative demeanor. All of this may contribute to a substantial decrease in the effectiveness of scientists and scholars in the context of their own countries.

But writing skills are by no means the only ones needed. In this age of scientific information explosion, when thick issues of scientific journals shower on a scientist almost daily, the mere magnitude of the written records of science makes it impossible for a scientist to rely on written modes of communication alone. Indeed, the importance of oral communication among scientists for the purpose of transmitting research results continually grows. Seminar lectures, talks at conferences, workshops, other types of meetings, and informal interaction during visits to scientific institutions are some of the opportunities for such oral communication.

Informal modes of communication are especially important when information is transmitted from the scientist to someone outside the sciences who is a potential user of the results. The written modes of communication are especially inadequate in such situations. For example, engineers, who do not read scientific journals, may not be able to understand or assess the importance of scientific reports written in scientific jargon. In contrast, oral communication, with an opportunity for instant feedback, can better serve in such situations.

3.2.8. To persuade

As mentioned earlier, scientific and scholarly results and ideas often encounter objections, critique, opposition, and competing ideas. Even if there is a method that, in the long run, can quite unambiguously discriminate the "right" from the "wrong," during this sorting process, discussions, debates, arguments, and confrontations are common, and, hence, the persuasive power of a scientist plays a significant role. In the scholarly world, persuasive power plays an even more important role.

Persuasive power is also essential in dealing with science administrators and policy makers. Science policy, even at its best, is very far from being a science, and, instead, it relies on empirical procedures, estimates and guesses, political considerations, and personal factors. Resources in science, even in the best system of science policy decisions, are allocated in part based on the promise the scientist shows in being able to produce valuable research in the future. Such promise cannot be evaluated by scientific means, but must be based on past performance and on the ability of the scientist to persuade the decision makers of his capability in the future. The situation is even more subjective and vague in the social sciences and the humanities, in which objective criteria for *a priori* evaluation and assessment are even more lacking.

3.3. The Duality of Linkages

For a scientist or scholar in a developing country, contacts and linkages are quite sharply divided into two categories: international and domestic. This sharp division exists because of the isolation that prevails in the developing countries and impedes contact with the outside world, making both written and person-to-person contacts with scientists and scholars outside the country difficult, intermittent, and delayed.

There is also another reason why such a sharp division exists. Since a developing country ordinarily produces only a very small fraction of the world's science and a correspondingly small fraction of scholarly knowledge, new ideas, trends, movements, research directions, and results are most likely to come from abroad. Thus, the nature of the interaction with people from abroad tends to be qualitatively different from the interaction with local colleagues.

Finally, there is a difference between the two kinds of linkages because the linkages to other countries tend to be mainly with other scientific and scholarly colleagues, while the domestic linkages are only partly with such colleagues. Local linkages also exist with the users of research, with the policy makers and managers of research, and with the population at large.

As we will see in section 3.4, all mechanisms of interaction with counterparts in other countries are stunted and weak for a scientist or scholar in a developing country. The communication patterns in the worldwide scientific community are, to a large extent, determined by the scientists themselves. Scientists control the publication patterns of scientific journals; the structuring, location, and list of participants of scientific meetings; the invitation of visitors; the itinerary for scientific visits; and the mailing lists of reports and preprints. It is, therefore, useful to ask how the worldwide scientific community determines these patterns.

On the whole, these patterns are governed by the scientists' desire to maximize the totality of research results in the *near* future. Scientists are eager to see as much progress in their fields of research as possible, and to see this during their lifetimes. Therefore, they are, on the whole, not very sensitive to long-range considerations. To be able to participate in and observe progress in the next five or ten years is the main focus of their attention.

In order to achieve this, the most effective policy appears to be to provide resources in generous fashion to those scientists who have produced the most research results in the recent past. If they were productive yesterday, they can also be expected to be productive tomorrow. From a different perspective, this is the principle that "the rich get richer, the poor get poorer." In a more literary vein, this is the Matthew Principle, stated in the Bible passage: "For to everyone who has will more be given, and he will have abundance; but from him who has not, even what he has will be taken away." Matthew 25:29.

Since science and scholarship in the developing countries are relatively young and small in size, their past record is generally modest. Indeed, over 90 percent of new scientific results in the world are produced by scientists from countries containing only one-fourth of the human population, while the other three-fourths of humanity supplies less than 10 percent. As a result, the resources for communication within the worldwide scientific community are given preferentially to those who are already well integrated into this community, and those who are left out (mainly those in the developing countries) continue to be left out.

The same situation prevails also in the community of scholars. From a long-term point of view, such a distribution of resources is harmful for worldwide science and scholarship, since it restricts the use of human brainpower to 25 percent efficiency. But, a more equitable distribution of resources would bring substantial results only some three or four decades from now, since it would take that long for the developing world to build up its scientific and scholarly production to the level now shown by the "advanced" countries, and such a long time horizon is outside the range of interest of most working scientists and scholars.

Thus, in interacting with the scientific and scholarly community outside the country, the scientist or scholar in a developing country is in a more difficult and disadvantageous position. One might think, however, that this would not hold for linkages *within* the country, since such linkages do not need substantial financial or material resources and they depend entirely on the researchers *within* the country. This expectation, however, is quite wrong; internal communication, the internal linkages and interactions within a developing country, is also very tenuous, very weak, very poorly developed, and very intermittent. Researchers in almost adjacent institutions hardly interact with each other, domestic journals are not very successful, local professional societies seldom go beyond ceremonial and social functions, and collaboration among researchers from the same country is weak.

There are many causes for this strange state of affairs. For one thing, the sociology of a small scientific or scholarly community differs from that of a large one (Lomnitz 1979). Personal animosities are more difficult to hide since avoiding the collision course is difficult when the community is small. The general frustrations of working in science or producing scholarship in developing countries also manifest themselves in the interpersonal relationships within the community. Also, the generation gap is often more hostile in the developing countries. In general, there are two different kinds of generation gaps. One stems from the fact that people at twenty-five generally have different world views, different values, different expectations, different interests, and different emotional lives than those at sixty-five. The second kind of generation gap originates in the fact that, at any given point in time, the twenty-five-year-olds and the sixty-five-year-olds were born in different eras and hence started off with different traditions, values, and world views. In developing countries, this second type of generation gap is exacerbated by the fact that the older generation had a more adverse educational and professional environment and, hence, less of an opportunity to evolve its talent and convert it into achievements. Thus, the younger generation often considers the older one inferior in talent and competence, while the older one complains about the ingratitude of the younger generation, which appears oblivious to the sacrifices the older generation made in order to prepare a better scientific and scholarly environment for their successors.

As mentioned earlier, linkages within the developing countries also include interaction with the users of research results. In the "advanced" countries, there is a traditional and well-developed mechanism for the transfer of research results into applications. This is not so in the developing countries. The link, for example, between engineers and the productive sector of the economy is similarly tenuous. Industry, whether owned by the local government or by transnational corporations, prefers to import foreign technology and production methods rather than to utilize indigenous resources. A scientist, therefore, can make enormous contributions to his own country by trying to bridge these gaps and by taking the initiative for interaction with the technologists and the technology users in his country.

Similarly, the scholar in a developing country must, by necessity, be the founder and nurturer of the intellectual class in his country. Such a group of intellectuals is likely to be small, ineffectual, and at odds with the more traditional leaders, whether political, religious, military, or bureaucratic (Alatas 1977; Shils 1961). The influence of the intellectuals in a society does not depend on their academic excellence alone, but also on their ability to affect their environment by persuasion, by teaching, and by action.

Finally, scientists and scholars must also have an effect on the population of the country as a whole. Their activities are justified in part by the cultural influence of their disciplines. Science, for example, has had an enormous effect on the world view of the average person in Western society over the past 300 years. Attitudes toward the nature of knowledge, toward what man can do to shape his fate, and toward change as an inevitable element in human development have been profoundly altered during that period of time.

In contrast, science has not yet had much impact as a cultural force in the developing countries (Basalla 1967). These countries may be inundated by the products of modern technology, but the thinking of the people has been little touched. Science, not as an entire culture, but as an important ingredient in any culture, is a crucial part of any development process, and it is the responsibility of the local practitioners of science to implant science into the local culture.

The modes for transmission of science into the mass culture are poorly used at the moment in many developing countries. Newspaper coverage of science is rare and of low quality, radio and television programs on science are ill developed, and exhibits and museums are seldom very successful. The reluctance and inability of local scientists to get involved in such activities is at least one reason for this state of affairs.

Finally, a scientist or a scholar in a developing country needs to interact well with those who make policy on science and higher learning. In most cases, policy makers will not come from the scientific or scholarly community, and they will have no personal experience with research. They are likely to come from the ranks of civil servants, whose education includes little, if any, contact with the natural sciences, and only a formalistic immersion into the world of the social sciences and humanities. The situation could be described, extending C.P. Snow's image, in terms of three cultures: that of the natural scientist and engineer, that of the social scientist and scholar in the humanities, and that of the rest of society. Decision makers are likely to come from the third culture. One might applaud this since, after all, they are representative of the country as a whole. But, at the same time, because of the huge differences in background and understanding, the policy makers need a great deal of interaction with the scientific and scholarly communities if they are to make decisions in the areas of science and learning that are realistic and helpful for the country's development.

And yet, this very-much-needed interaction in the developing countries is also weak. The scientific and scholarly communities, in general, fail to take the opportunity to initiate and carry out a dialogue with the policy makers, with the result that those policies that are put into effect often tend to be counterproductive, despite the best intentions on the part of the policy makers.

In summary, a scientist or a scholar in a developing country tends to have weak communication links both with the international scientific and scholarly community, and with domestic groups including other scientists and scholars, the users of research information, the people as a whole, and the policy makers. It is both in the self-interest of the scientist or scholar and in the interest of the country as a whole to put considerable effort into strengthening these ties.

3.4. Mechanisms of Interaction

This section summarizes the various mechanisms and the variety of tools that are used in the interaction of scientists and of scholars. This discussion thus complements section 3.3, which discusses the initiators and the recipients in communicative links.

Two other chapters of this book offer material that is also relevant to this topic. Chapter 6 deals with libraries, and chapter 2, with alumni as a mechanism for interaction. The present discussion is complementary to that in those two chapters.

The tools of communication can be readily divided into two types: written and oral.

3.4.1. Written modes of communication

In both scientific work and scholarly endeavors, the written modes of communication are essential, though there are some differences in detail between the two areas. These differences originate in some epistemological and structural differences between scientific research and scholarly pursuits. In particular, science (meaning only the natural and not the social sciences) visibly grows as time goes on; progress in science can be discerned and quantified more easily, and it is cumulative. Therefore, a piece of scientific research has much greater timeliness and is much more "urgent" than a piece of scholarship. For this reason, the sciences place very high value on speedy publication, speedy communication, speedy transmittal of results.

The second characteristic of science, as distinct from the social sciences and humanities, is its terseness of language. Especially in the highly developed and very quantitative and mathematical sciences such as physics, but even in the more qualitative and less well developed areas such as biology, the results of one "unit" of research (a concept admittedly not too well defined) can usually be transmitted on ten printed pages. In contrast, in the social sciences or humanities, there is no special and condensed language to communicate in, and, in fact, the skillful, powerful, and often lengthy use of common language to persuade is an essential part of communication. As a consequence, ten printed pages rarely suffice to communicate the results of a "unit" of research in the social sciences, and 50 or 500 pages are often required.

The result of this difference is that in the natural sciences journals are far ahead of books in importance, while in the social sciences and humanities, if the two modes are not equally important, it is books that may be more important. Thus, the requirements for written modes of communication are substantially different for scientists than for scholars.

Nevertheless, in the developing countries scholars and scientists face similar problems, because access to both books and journals is difficult. Both are generally published in the advanced countries, and they are extremely expensive, even by the standards of those countries themselves. A scientific book nowadays costs about fifteen to twenty cents per page, an amount at least five times what it costs to photocopy a page. Furthermore, books must be paid for in hard currency. Journals are bulky and, therefore, their air shipment over large distances is costly. Additionally, many journals have a dual subscription rate: a relatively low (and subsidized) one for individuals and a very high rate for libraries. Because most subscribers in developing countries are libraries, this puts an extra burden on those countries.

In the case of books, special arrangements have occasionally been made, in cooperation with the original publisher, for issuing inexpensive "international editions" that are then made available only in developing countries. No similar arrangements have so far been made for journals, since the publishers of journals (whether they are nonprofit professional societies or commercial organizations) have refused to grant permission for such satellite editions. Only concerted pressure from scientists and scholars from the developing countries will ever overcome this opposition.

Another approach is, of course, to establish publishers in the developing countries themselves. This would require a spirit of energetic private entrepreneurship (for which there is seldom a tradition) and skill in areas such as publishing technology, distribution, and advertising. During the past two or three years at least one such publisher has become established. This publisher not only has contributed to the distribution of scientific books in the developing countries, but has also been hailed in the advanced countries for the topical and relatively inexpensive volumes of high quality that it has produced. This is the World Scientific Publishing Company of Singapore, the creation of a group of scientists. More such enterprises would be most welcome.

Problems exist not only with current issues of journals, but also with previous issues, or back volumes. When a new library is established in a developing country, the task of purchasing back volumes of scientific and scholarly journals is enormous. Both scholars and scientists rely heavily on journals, but, because the material deposited in scholarly journals "ages" more slowly, the library has to go back farther in time for those journals than it does for scientific journals. Back volumes are often out of print, and, in any case, are very expensive. In the sciences, a program has been established under which scientists in the advanced countries can donate the back issues of their own journal subscriptions to institutions in developing countries, with the cost of shipping paid for by the donor or by the recipient, or, if neither can do so, by the program itself. The coordinator of this program is H.R. Dalafi, at the International Centre of Theoretical Physics, Miramare 34100, Trieste, Italy.

The sense of urgency in the sciences has created an additional channel of written communication, that of prepublication reports or preprints. They are distributed by the author to a mailing list of his own choosing, which usually is abundant in Nobel prize winners and short on addresses in developing countries. The importance of preprints varies with the research field. In some of the frontier fields of science, preprints constitute the predominant mode of written communication, and the journals are relegated to purely archival functions.

With the fast growing mass of facts, tables, data, and quantitative parametrizations in the sciences, there is a corresponding increase in computerized information systems, providing not only factual details, but also assistance in locating references and relevant material in the ocean of scientific information. The value of these computerized systems for scientists and scholars in the developing countries has been slight, for several reasons. First, locating factual details is only a small aspect of scientific research and is often not very important. Second, such high-technology machinery is very vulnerable to deficiencies in local technological conditions, such as lack of repair facilities for computers, fluctuations in voltage, and power outages. Third, the organization of such facilities in developing countries is often very rigid and bureaucratic, so that while the signal may come easily from Paris, for example, over thousands of miles to the local receptor machine, the transmission of the information over the last 10 or 100 miles, from the local receptor machine to the potential user, may be full of obstacles. It is well for a scientist or scholar who returns to his developing country from abroad not to count on much of these complex information systems, but instead to rely more on the more conventional written modes of communication, together with oral modes.

3.4.2. Oral modes of communication

As earlier stated, we are facing the seeming paradox that the larger the scientific and scholarly communities become, the greater the relative importance of the oral means of communication as compared with the written ones. Regrettably, the developing countries are even more handicapped in this realm than they are in the written modes. The most visible oral mode of communication among scientists and among scholars is the conference. There are hundreds of scientific and scholarly meetings and conferences every year around the world. They are generally held in scientifically or scholastically active and well developed countries, because, in those countries, there are tested expertise and facilities for holding such meetings, and because the total transportation expense can be minimized that way. Scientists and scholars from developing countries are greatly inconvenienced by this way of determining the location of meetings, since they, having few resources to begin with, must travel long distances and pay for very expensive accommodations.

Since researchers from the developing countries have lower visibility anyway (for reasons discussed earlier), they may not be so readily invited to meetings in the first place. Moreover, because scientific events are not likely to occur in the developing countries, the frequent travels of the

The Scientist or Scholar

worldwide scientific community take it much more often into the "advanced" countries than into the developing world. Thus, scientists and scholars in the developing world receive personal visits from the colleagues abroad only on rare occasions.

A nearly costless and simple program can be helpful in increasing such visits. In each scientific or scholarly discipline in a general geographic area, an information exchange can be established to forward information about impending travels by scientists into that area to institutions in that area who are interested in receiving visitors. With that information, the institutions can approach the potential travelers, if they wish, to persuade them to make stopovers during their trips.

The lack of personal visits could be compensated for by enhanced personal interaction of scientists within the country. As mentioned earlier, however, this does not take place, and, two scientists or scholars, working within a few miles of each other in a developing country, are much less likely to interact than two similar persons in a well-developed country.

A most commonly used and very helpful tool of person-to-person communication is the telephone. It is often much more advantageous for a scientist, instead of spending half an hour in a nearby library to locate some information, to telephone another scientist, perhaps 2,000 miles away, who knows the answer. It is faster, cheaper, and more reliable. Communication by telephone is even more advantageous when the piece of information is not just a matter of "fact" but of opinion, experience, intutition, concepts. With the rapidly decreasing rates for international calls, the use of the phone can be further extended.

But, use of the telephone can be depended on only in the advanced countries. In the developing countries, typically, even the domestic phone system is marginal. The connections are poor, few people have phones, and intercity calls are clumsy. To make international calls is even more difficult, and it is also very expensive by local standards. Thus, the telephone, a most useful tool of communication, is relegated to very minor importance in those countries.

To compensate for this, is out to be possible to use shortwave radio for international scientific communication. Shortwave radio sets are relatively inexpensive, and the network of shortwave communications is, therefore, greatly decentralized and individualized. There are private sets in the hands of "radio buffs" everywhere, and many of them would be happy to contribute time on their sets for scientific or scholarly communication. To make this network function in the service of such communication, however, scientists and scholars themselves would have to do a bit of organizational work. This has not been done so far.

3.5. Creating Opportunities for Professional Interaction

The foregoing discussion simply provided a background, an analysis of the situation, and list of problems to be faced and overcome. This section, the most important part of this chapter, summarizes what needs to be done in the face of these problems to assure the scientist or scholar a functional system of professional interactions, contacts, and communication channels.

In a functional sense, the discussion can be divided easily into two parts. The first deals with what can be done while the student from the developing country is receiving advanced education in the United States. The second part then summarizes action that can be taken after the student has returned home.

3.5.1. During the period of education abroad

The first step during the student's education in the United States is to become aware of and acquainted with the problems of communication and interaction in the home country. It is extremely difficult for the student to acquire this awareness, since not only did he learn nothing about these problems while acquiring a less advanced degree in his home country, but the American educational system will probably teach him nothing about these problems either.

To understand why this is the case, it is important to realize that, naturally enough, the American educational system is geared primarily toward the perceived needs of American students. Since these students, upon receiving their degrees, generally obtain positions in an already established scientific or scholarly infrastructure, their initial duties involve only scientific research and teaching or scholarly work and teaching. The formation and maintenance of the infrastructure in which they are absorbed is taken care of by their more experienced colleagues. Only later in their careers will these young scientists and scholars be called upon to help manage the infrastructure itself. Specifically, at the beginning of their careers, they will be able to use the generally well developed channels of professional communication, interaction, and contact. Thus, it is thought unnecessary to teach American students about these infrastructural or contextual aspects of science and scholarship, and such considerations are therefore not part of advanced education in the United States.

Unfortunately, however, the student from the developing country does not return to such a developed infrastructure, and, in particular, he does not return to a functioning system of professional interactions, contacts, and linkages. He will, therefore, have to perform a double task after his return: carry out scientific research or scholarly work and create the circumstances under which science and scholarship can be practiced. The student will have received no training at all for this second task during his education in the United States, unless he acquires it on his own in an extracurricular way.

Suggestions and proposals have been made for American universities to provide some supplemental education to students from the developing countries in these contextual and auxiliary aspects of science and scholarship. One possible way to do this is in the framework of a special centralized summer program for such students. This was tried for the first time in the summer of 1983, on a small scale, under a pilot project in Antigonish, Nova Scotia, organized by J. William McGowan of the University of Western Ontario and held for students from Asian countries. The second way to develop supplemental education would be to utilize the local expertise at each university department to expose students, in an informal way (perhaps through reading courses), to these infrastructural considerations. Neither of these modes can, however, be relied on at the moment, and thus the student himself has to initiate contact with faculty members who can help him build up some awareness and acquaintance with these problems.

The next step, somewhat related to the first one, is to try to get some practical experience, in addition to the regular curriculum, in matters related to these infrastructural problems of science and higher learning, particularly those related to communication, contacts, and professional integration. There might be opportunities to assist in publishing professional journals, organizing scientific conferences, managing professional societies, arranging for outside visitors to the department, managing the flow of preprints to a research group in the department, setting up exhibits in the local science museum, ordering research equipment from outside suppliers, dealing with the management of the local machine shops, and similar infrastructural activities. Any experience with and insight into the practical aspects of these activities would be of great value to the student.

Perhaps the most valuable and important action the student can undertake during his advanced education in the United States is building up personal ties within the professional community. However, most students from developing countries are not naturally inclined to devote much time and effort to this task while in the United States. They tend to come from societies in which the relationship between students, on the one hand, and professors, professionals, and elders in general, on the other hand, is much more distant and formal than in the United States. Students therefore tend to stay silent and in the background unless they are spoken to or approached. Furthermore, these students tend to concentrate strictly on their formal studies, which, in addition to the general problems of living in a strange society and a strange country, consume most of their time and attention.

A special determination and effort are therefore necessary for these students to build up personal ties in the professional community. Talking informally with faculty, developing comradeships with fellow students, befriending scientists and scholars visiting the department, and spending vacations visiting other universities and research centers are all means to accomplish the goal. Seeds sown on such occasions will turn out to be invaluable years later when these ties will represent the cracks in the isolating wall surrounding the scientist or scholar.

It would be helpful if faculty at American universities recognized this opportunity and encouraged and helped the foreign students under their supervision to utilize it. In general, this is not likely to occur, and thus it is the student himself who will have to take the initiative.

More formal links with professional societies can be established during the years of education. Most such societies, in an effort to attract students, have discount membership fees and special activities for such students.

3.5.2. After returning home

It is clear from the foregoing discussion that, when the student returns home, he has a long list of actions awaiting him. With respect to communication abroad, he will have to fight for access to scientific journals, he will have to assure his place on preprint mailing lists, he will have to monitor the local library for the acquisition of back journals and books, he will have to try to participate in international conferences, he will have to campaign for the worldwide scientific and scholarly communitiy to pay greater attention to his country and the others in the developing world, and he will have to keep an ear open for potential visitors who plan to overfly his country but could be persuaded to interrupt their trips for visits. The returned student will also have to interact with editors of international journals when submitting papers of his own, he will want to explore the possibility of collaborative research projects, and he may want to explore the local opportunities for shortwave radio communication abroad. This agenda alone would suffice for a decade or two, but added to it must be efforts to improve domestic communication.

The newly trained professional will want to intensify the meager interaction patterns between scientists or scholars within the country, arrange visits to other institutions for lectures, and revitalize the interactive patterns between the generators of knowledge and the users of it. He will want to devote some effort toward spreading the attitudes and results of science and culture among the population as a whole, he will want to interact with policy makers and with the leaders of the country in general, and he may want to contribute to the local professional societies and journals. These are only a sampling of the activities on another agenda that is long enough for a lifetime.

It is clear that no person could tend to all these aspects of interaction and communication simultaneously. Indeed, it is much better to select one or two areas and devote persistent, concentrated, and patient effort to them

The Scientist or Scholar

over a long period of time. The individual must decide for himself which of these tasks harmonize best with his interests and which are particularly urgent and important, and this decision must be made usually only after he has returned home and had an opportunity to survey the local scene. There are many ways the scientist or scholar can live up to the responsibility of being a scientist or scholar while carrying out responsibilities to himself, his family, his discipline, his society, and his fellow humans the world over. To make an intelligent choice, however, he needs an overview of the whole spectrum, and this volume is an attempt to contribute to this overview.

3.6. Epilogue

Establishing science and scholarship in a country is a long-range activity, taking decades and several generations of scientists and scholars. It is a task which sometimes appears excruciatingly slow, or even at a standstill, but which shows definite progress if viewed in intervals of five to ten years. To promote such progress, it must be recognized that science and scholarship are not formal sets of abstract knowledge, but they are activities in which people engage themselves. If people are in fact to do this, they need an appropriate environment, important features of which are interaction, communication, and linkages. Indeed, isolation is one of the most deadly enemies of progress in the developing countries. An interactive environment does not come about by itself. Those people who wish to thrive in such an environment are precisely those who must create it. What the necessary elements of such an environment are and what can be done to create them is something a student must learn during his education. Although we are a long way from making this an automatic part of the education of all students in the developing countries, through discussions such as those in this volume, these students may be stimulated to invest some time and effort into the creation of an interactive environment and, thereby, to reap its benefits throughout their professional careers.

References Cited

Alatas, S.H. 1977. *Intellectuals in developing societies.* London: Frank Cass.

Basalla, George. 1967. The spread of western science. *Science* 156: 611–622.

Lomnitz, Larissa. 1979. Hierarchy and peripherality: The organization of a Mexican research institute. *Minerva* 17: 527–548.

Moravcsik, Michael J. 1980. *How to grow science.* New York: Universe Books.

Salam, Abdus. 1966. The isolation of the scientist in developing countries. *Minerva* 4: 461–465.

Shils, Edward. 1966. *The intellectual between tradition and modernity: The Indian situation.* The Hague: Mouton.

Bibliography

Dart, Francis, et al. 1975. Observations on an obstacle course. *International Educational and Cultural Exchange* 11(2): 29-40.

Eisemon, Thomas. 1982. *The science profession in the Third World.* New York: Praeger.

Glyde, Henry. 1974. Insitutional links in science and technology: The United Kingdom and Thailand. *International Development Review Focus* 15: 7-11.

Moravcsik, Michael J. 1976. *Science development: The building of science in less developed countries.* Bloomington, Ind.: PASITAM.

Morgan, Robert P. 1979. *Science and technology for development.* New York: Pergamon.

Pyenson, Lewis. 1978. The incomplete transmission of a European image: Physics at Greater Buenos Aires and Montreal, 1890-1920. *Proceedings of the American Philosophical Society* 122(2): 92-114.

Roche, Marcel. 1976. Early history of science in Spanish America. *Science* 194: 806-821.

Sabato, Jorge. 1970. Quantity versus quality in scientific research (1): The special case of developing countries. *Impact* 20: 183-197.

Wijesekera, R.O.B. 1976. Scientific research in a small developing nation— Sri Lanka. *Scientific World* 1: 6-11.

Zahlan, A.B. 1980. *Science and science policy in the Arab world.* New York: St. Martin's.

4.

The Professional Integration of Women*

Mary Joy Pigozzi
Patricia W. Barnes-McConnell
Sally K. Williams

4.1. Introduction

This book examines various aspects of integration into a professional career. Here we look specifically at the professional integration of women. We are assuming there are significant differences between women's professional environments and those of their male counterparts that can be traced to gender. We begin our discussion by examining the professional environment; that is, the combination of social and cultural conditions that influence and surround one as a professional. In addressing this, we have tried to separate out various influences so as to analyze them and see how they might be individually important. We recognize fully that it is most likely that several of these conditions may affect the professional in combination and that they may simultaneously be acting on, and therefore having an effect on, one another. As every professional environment surrounds a person, we next focus on that person through a consideration of marginality, tokenism, and individual advancement. Next, we look at some significant factors surrounding women preparing themselves to be professionals while they are in the United States. A final section is a view to the future, recognizing the gains women have made and acknowledging the challenges and opportunities that new and unknown environments will offer professional women.

---
*This chapter is dedicated to Marilyn Parkhurst who brought the authors together and whose untimely death made it impossible for her to contribute.

4.2. Understanding the Professional Environment

There are many ways a professional environment can be bounded or described. In our opinion there is at the core of every professional environment an individual—a human being with particular goals, principles, and values that will determine, in part, how that individual functions in the various roles and responsibilities he or she assumes throughout a professional life. But, human beings do not function in a vacuum, regardless of the positions they asume. Every individual is linked to other individuals, groups, or organizations and structures and these also influence, in varying degrees, professional performance. In this part of the chapter, we raise questions and identify issues regarding the female professional and factors in her professional environment that have a significant impact because of her gender.* These environmental factors include formal and informal professional networks, personal networks, familial and other personal responsibilities, and selected aspects of the organization in which the female professional works.

4.2.1. Networks

In general terms, a network consists of individuals and organizations who are voluntarily linked in a communications web. Network participants are such by choice and there are good reasons for this. Networks serve to link individuals who have common interests and concerns. One of the most important aspects of the linking role of networks is that they assist individuals in overcoming a sense of isolation. In this regard, networks can be especially important to women, who may feel doubly isolated—as professionals and as women in their professions. Many networks do not have "rules" or "entry requirements"—networkers are quite free to have their own opinions and to "drop into" or "drop out of" the network at any time. But, to be part of a network, one must participate in some way. This might be through sharing ideas or exchanging information, for example. As a phenomenon, networking is not new (Global networks 1982). There are many kinds of networks. Some, such as the Transnational Network of Appropriate Alternative Technologies (TRANET 1982) are very focused. Others, such as the women and food network *(The Women and Food Information Network Newsletter* 1982) or the nonformal education network (Information for development 1982), might be more general. Still others are very specific to a particular individual and, in this chapter, we shall focus on this last type. That is, we shall look at the people and organizations who, because of shared interests and concerns, have relevance to the professional woman.

---

*In doing so, we realize that many of the issues and questions we raise may also be quite appropriate for individuals who represent, for example, different cultures or ethnic groups, minority groups, and minority philosophical approaches in the workplace.

4.2.1.1. Professional networks

Professional networks are the web of people and institutions to whom female professionals look for support, ideas, assistance, and professional critique related to work performance. A student enrolled in a U.S. institution has a professional network on and off campus. This includes her adviser and any other scholars with whom she works or actively discusses common interests. Fellow students with whom she interacts professionally are also a part of the network. In addition, there are colleagues who have become important professional links through professional societies, conferences, and workshops. A student who comes to the university from a professional position in her home country can add the professional contacts from her U.S. experience to her existing professional network (colleagues and coworkers from her home country, for example). This is covered in more detail in section 4.4.

Over time, then, a professional network may continue to grow and change, a desirable feature since a person is likely to have changing interests, responsibilities, and roles over the course of a professional life. There may be associations to which one "should" belong because they represent organizations of scholars in a particular field. There are other links that may be useful to the professional woman that are less obvious. Asking colleagues, reading publications in related fields, and pursuing personal contacts are among the ways a woman might find others who are engaged in similar work.

It is possible that professional associations in a particular field of study do not exist in the home country, or even the region. If this is the case, it might be advantageous for the female student to consider how she might organize links with others engaged in similar kinds of work in the home country and to consider what kinds of skills and information she might need to establish such an organization.

Frequently, professional organizations do exist in the home country. In preparing to return, female students may wish to consider how they will relate to these associations. Having had the opportunity to study overseas recently, an individual may be in a position to bring fresh ideas to the association and to provide in-country members with additional links to potential colleagues in the international arena. Breaking into a new group, especially if there are no or few female members, may be particularly difficult, however. There may also be problems in dealing with association activities. For example, new ideas or concerns about the "appropriateness" of association activities (such as questioning activities that reinforce negative stereotypes of women) may not be welcomed by those who have dedicated time and energy to maintaining the association. Thus, it becomes important to both the association and the professional for the professional to consider how and when involvement is likely to be beneficial—as well as what kinds of involvement would be best.

Integration of Women

Obviously, this kind of consideration is not limited to involvement in a professional association but to all potential links in the professional environment. One goal might be to work toward the development of a supportive professional network that gives access to those involved in related scholarly work, information, and professional development opportunities (such as training and travel). Because it is often difficult for a woman to move into male-dominated milieux on her own, the professional network can serve as an entree and to "legitimize" the female as a professional so that she can actively participate in all aspects of her profession.

4.2.1.2. Personal networks

We have suggested that a sense of isolation is common among professionals and that often women feel especially isolated because of their gender. There are many reasons for the relationship between gender and a sense of isolation. For example, fewer women than men are selected to engage in overseas training (often as a result of the sponsoring agencies' practices). And, in many countries women have less access to educational opportunities so those women who have received higher education abroad are in a minority. As a result, professional women may feel "alone" upon their return and find that there are few or no women who have had similar experiences, either as students overseas or as students who have returned after an extended absence from home. Experience has shown that building a "personal" network or a support group around significant characteristics such as shared values and goals can often assist the female professional in fighting the sense of isolation and provide new sources for finding solutions to problems.

The personal network consists of other individuals who can provide support to the professional, but in a more personal way than does the professional network. Participants in this network may or may not have a similar professional expertise. If professional isolation, in terms of subject matter, is a reality for the female professional, it is likely that her personal network will be made up of persons from other walks of life. Individuals in a personal network are usually able to empathize, to understand at least some of the situations being faced, and to assist with analyzing problems and suggesting solutions. For example, a soil scientist might find that the person who understands her professional situation best is a person who works in the Bureau of Statistics—they may share a common experience of overseas training and of being the only highly placed woman in a ministry.

Sometimes it is very easy to form bonds of friendship with other professionals, thus developing a base of personal support. In situations where there are few female professionals, forging these bonds with other women who have similar outlooks on professionalism and professional advancement can provide a "critical mass"—a group that is large enough that its concerns cannot be ignored. As a woman develops a personal network within the professional setting, it is important for her to consider her assumptions. For example, it may be inaccurate to attribute loneliness to gender alone. There are many male colleagues who are very supportive of female professionals. Conversely, it is equally important to remember that not all women share the same concerns, are similarly motivated, or would automatically become a member of the personal network.

4.2.2. Familial and personal responsibilities

Personal relationships also influence the woman and her professional environment. Friendship and kinship ties provide needed love and support. But they also place demands on the woman's time such that she may feel a tension between her personal and professional responsibilities. Frequently, a woman finds that it takes extra skill and energy to balance the various roles she may be expected to play (daughter, highly placed government official, wife, mother, and chair of local organization, for example). In preparing to return to the home country, an individual may wish to consider questions such as the following: Are family members likely to have difficulty accepting my new multiple roles? What kind of spouse is likely to be supportive of me as a professional? How easy is it going to be to find a spouse? Will there be acceptable employment for me and for my spouse? Is there likely to be help available for household responsibilities? Experience shows that professional women have to face these issues and that concerns regarding marriage and maintaining good marital relations are of paramount importance to single women who are studying in the United States (Boakari 1982; Parkhurst 1982). Unfortunately, there is no single set of responses to these concerns. Having given thought to the issues, however, often makes reentry after study abroad a little easier to understand.

4.2.3. Organizational structure

Conditions centered around the structure of the organization and how that structure defines and responds to the women in it can also affect a woman in the professional setting. First, it is worth considering the professional responsibilities of a female employee. Often, successful women find themselves in managerial positions. Yet, their academic training may not have provided them with relevant skills. To complicate matters, it is frequently boy children rather than girl children who are socialized to handle managerial responsibilities in other settings. To compensate, women may wish to consider if it is possible to use the existing organizational structure to gain additional skills. For example, participating in committees might enable one to get a different perspective on people and procedures in the organization.

A critical part of the professional environment relates to communication within the organization. In almost every organization there are both formal and informal communication links. Formal links are usually easy to identify, as they relate directly to the formal structure of the organization. Informal links can be much more problematic and may be much more important than the formal ones. Access to the informal communication network in an organization may be especially difficult for women if they are a distinct minority in the organization. For example, if business decisions are made over lunch at a restaurant where it is inappropriate for women to go, or where they may go only with a personal male escort, then the female professional is faced with a difficult situation. Even if the situation is not this severe, traditional gender relationships may make access to, and acceptance in, these very important informal communications networks harder than one might otherwise expect. A female professional may find that one of her most significant sources of information is the wives of her male colleagues rather than the colleagues themselves, and this fact suggests the extreme sensitivity of her position.

The female professional may also wish to consider how gender affects the professional environment outside specific professional responsibilities. In this regard, it is important to have a sense of what other colleagues and "the organization" expect from a female professional. One way to focus on this is to identify the roles and positions that have previously been held by women in the organization. If a relatively large number of women have held high positions in the organization, the addition of one woman to the professional staff may not be a particularly notable event. In other situations, the addition of a female professional may be a new occurrence and may result in stress on the new employee and on those who work with her. This stress may be due to coworkers' lack of experience in working with women, insecurity, or colleagues' assumptions that the woman will not be able to perform sufficiently well. The woman may have to come to terms with being stereotyped into a traditional female role. For example, if her male colleagues cannot accept her professional contributions when she refuses to combine them with such tasks as making coffee or taking the minutes, she will have to decide if it is in her best interest to refuse the traditional role outright or adapt, adjust, or compromise.

Sometimes a woman finds herself in the position of being what is needed in order for there to be a "critical mass" of individuals who are interested in articulating concerns relating to women. This may place the new worker in the difficult position of being pulled in different ways by various interest groups in the organization. Often, a woman finds herself placed in a situation where she is the voice of all women, expected to articulate the concerns of all women. In many cases, a woman may sense that one of the reasons she has been employed is to fulfill an unwritten "quota" of female employees, that she is there as a token, a concept discussed below.

Many other possibilities can emerge as a woman examines the roles and actions that are expected of her above and beyond the substantive area of her job. What is important is that the professional woman acknowledge the presence of these expectations, attempt to understand how they affect her professional environment, and, then, carry out her professional responsibilities with this in mind.

4.3. Tokenism, Marginality, and Individual Advancement

We shall address the phenomena of marginality, tokenism, and individual advancement from the perspective of the person at the center of the professional environment. In many respects, the problems that have been discussed so far can be considered dimensions of marginality. It is an important factor in building and maintaining professional and personal networks, as well as in familial and personal responsibilities.

For the purposes of this chapter, the term marginality refers to those feelings and self-perceptions that emerge from within the individual in response to internal and external pressures toward exclusion. We consider it an "inside out" phenomenon. Tokenism refers to an assigned position of "tolerated stranger" that is based on the definition of the dominant group's characteristics. Thus, the dominant group perceives and treats the token as a representative of a group characteristically different from themselves. Tokenism is, therefore, a phenomenon that may be considered as coming from the "outside in." The token feels marginal, on the periphery, having only some of the dominant characteristics valued by the group while having to reconcile other, less valued and sometimes conflicting, characteristics. The professional placed in a situation of having to deal with these forces attempts to maintain a sense of equilibrium and searches for a route to individual advancement based on personal values and available resources.

The female professional finds her task of individual advancement especially difficult because of the power in the universal perception of the one and only characteristic that she shares with all other members of the group with which she is immediately identified—gender. This characteristic is usually conceptualized as "sex," with all of its connotations; it usually carries strong social role expectations with well known sanctions for role violations and generally overrides all other characteristics as the variable used to judge persons in initial social encounters.

4.3.1. Tokenism

One way to attempt to understand the situation in which professional women find themselves is through an examination of the concept of stranger, because professional women are frequently "strangers" in their organizations. The scholarly exploration of the concept of stranger, begun early in this century by Georg Simmel (1921, 1950), has made an important contribution to the understanding of the role of the "different" person in any group. Building on this early work, Shack and Skinner (1979) acknowledge the significance of the numbers of strangers versus the strength of the dominant group. Apparently, large numbers of strangers brought into a group tend to be more threatening to group members than smaller numbers, especially if the governing body is weak. Holding the strangers to a small representative or token number, therefore, has the important benefit of minimizing the threat.

One could ask, then, why allow any strangers into a group? According to Simmel, strangers are a positive element in group unification, self-definition, and growth. Also important is their role in communication diffusion. Outsiders bring new knowledge and values that can be used creatively by the existing group to construct new directions and strategies. Strong leaders, through the acceptance of strangers, are able to avoid the stagnation and decline frequently resulting from in-bred, homogeneous groups.

Another reason for the acceptance of a limited number of strangers is to ensure that only a controlled number of them are allowed to participate. It is felt that large numbers of such persons on the outside protesting is potentially destructive. The admission of a token from among organized strangers is a significant way to control their potential threat to the social order without having them take over leadership.

Thus, there are several elements reinforcing the maintenance of a token number of female professionals. As Kanter's work (1977) emphasizes, and we have discussed earlier in this chapter, it is important to the tokens that they expand their numbers, building a "critical mass." But, three factors operate to keep the number of tokens small, Kanter argues: Tokens are visible, their differences tend to be exaggerated by others, and generalizations about them are stereotyped. These factors force professional women, like all tokens, to face performance pressures. As tokens, these women are constantly in the public view; the long-range consequences of their behavior are overstressed, they must out-perform others for their competence to be noticed, and, thus, they are often in a position of fearing retaliation for outshining superiors. Performance pressures are often exacerbated because others are compelled to show off their perceived superiority, jokes are made about the token's group, abnormal deference to the token's difference is given constantly, tokens are physically avoided, and tokens are administered loyalty tests or made to give signs that they are more one of the dominant group than the group from which they came. Moreover, regardless of her position, the token is responded to in terms of a stereotype. For example, Parkhurst (1982) found that women from developing countries pursuing advanced education, training, or employment in the United States expressed resentment and frustration because it was often assumed that they could not speak English or that their vocabulary was limited.

The implications of these three factors (visibility, exaggerated differences, and stereotyping) are particularly poignant when one considers that cultures traditionally pretrain the female, long before professional school is begun, to be deferential to others, to be nurturing and self-sacrificing even when, or perhaps especially when, it is against her own best interest. Going against that force can exact a severe toll.

This analysis of the role and function of tokenism suggests that the professional put in the position of token can take the following steps to cope with the situation:

1. Identify the stereotypes, assumptions, and expectations of others.

2. Separate the stereotypes, assumptions, and expectations that are relevant to the job from those that are irrelevant.

3. Assess the extent to which the relevant stereotypes, assumptions, and expectations are realistic.

4. Map out strategies for working with those that are relevant and realistic, for diffusing those that are relevant and unrealistic, and for dismissing the others.

4.3.2. Marginality

Marginality, or a sense of being on the periphery, can be recognized when three things become clear. First, one cannot return to the original group as the same person, although still an acknowledged member of that group. Second, it is impossible to completely disengage from that group either by choice or circumstance. Third, because of original group membership it is impossible to become completely assimilated into a new group. The female professional, like other perceived outsiders, must learn to handle the conflict inherent in recognizing marginality. Stonequist (1961) suggests that there are three stages in marginality. He argues that, initially, individuals lack an awareness of conflict, then they become aware and consciously in conflict, and, finally, they make a creative adjustment to the conflict.

Persons aspiring to professional careers are often unaware of the potential conflicts that become visible only after moving far enough into the professional role to interact with the subtle rules, expectations, and dynamics among the organization's members. The creative adjustment required to resolve the conflict and become even a token member of the new group changes persons such that, as the common expression goes, "they can never go home again." In significant ways the old reference group is

Integration of Women

never quite the same. For example, both the married and the single women in the Parkhurst (1982) sample expressed sadness because they were so far away from their families, a distance they took to mean more than geographical distance. They felt there were experiences that they would never be able to share because those at home could not fully comprehend them.

Does the phenomenon of marginality make a useful contribution in a culture? Marginality experienced by a small number of persons in a society, like the presence of token strangers, serves a very important function. Stonequist (1961) points out that it is in the thinking and ponderings of persons who straddle different cultures and conceptual ideas that interpenetration is achieved, cross-cultural conflicts are resolved, and resources are fused. Acting out the new perceptions can change the culture in constructive ways. This reinforces the importance of marginal people, especially in rapidly changing societies.

Female professionals can be considered among the "persistent peoples" (Castile and Kushner 1981) who support the continuity of their original cultures over time while concurrently facilitating social change (Moone 1981). But the transition period, as they move into this role, is frequently fraught with fear of the unknown and forebodings which are exaggerated to the extent that the females were socialized to accept permissive and subordinate status. Those who aspire to greater independence have already made a certain commitment to marginality. They deliberately move across the grain of the socialized pattern; they physically move away from the close protection and support of their families. Frequently, it is with great trepidation that a woman gives in to hidden desires to use natural talent and intelligence, and thus it is with considerable ambivalence that she perceives the costs involved in taking control of her own life. Moving into the larger world, the woman senses an erosion of the old values. She loses the sense of community based on traditional dependence, first on her father, then on her husband or brother, and finally, late in life, on her son. The minimum consequences to be resolved—anxiety, ambiguity of self, and loneliness—set up an inner stress and need for self-justification.

4.3.3. Individual advancement

Reconciling the stress from within and the conflict imposed from without is possible to the extent that the woman has identified her own basic values and the range of personal and professional resources available for use. For example, she must ask, "What are my long-range personal and career goals? Why do I want to enter the profession? How do I anticipate my profession will help me reach these goals? What do I value the most in life?"

Also to be asked are questions regarding personal strengths and weaknesses, support services necessary and available in the environment, and the existence of potential allies and uncultivated friends. This latter dimension is particulary significant, for women in many cultures are socialized to see other women more as competitors than as potential friends—a situation that reinforces the isolation of female tokens and frequently results in counterproductive hostile behavior.

Acknowledgment of personal values and available resources brings the woman consciously to the exploration of options and, ultimately, to personal decision making (either by deliberate choice or by the default of inaction). The issue of choice, while often the most difficult for females socialized for permanent dependency, is also the most supportive of real independence. It is assumed that women moving toward greater professional involvement have taken at least the first painful steps in that direction. Assessing both the costs (that which must be given up in the short run and in the long run) and the benefits (that which is to be gained in the short run and in the long run) at each decision point prepares her to accept the hard answers that emerge.

Individual advancement means coming to appreciate and make use of the variables that accompany marginality—rights (i.e., to be a little different, to say the unusual), responsibilities (i.e., to those not so free, to those affected by group decisions), and power (i.e., in the broadened insight, in the ability to stand alone as the person who dares to be different and thus, by definition, is a potential leader and threat to the status quo). The female professional is able to make constructive use of these variables to the extent that she is able to—

- accept marginality—in essence, a loner, a maverick, someone who is "different";
- establish a personal sense of self—accept the self with all of the perceived strengths and weaknesses, including sexuality;
- commit herself to the chosen roles and their rules—fulfill the duties and live with the conflict in setting priorities;
- develop stress and tension outlets—recognize that these are particularly important following the inevitable failures that may be exaggerated if the woman is in constant public view;
- maintain a private realm or retreat—recognize the particular kind of stress constant public visibility carries.

In a way, through tokenism society awkwardly empowers individuals to use the energy generated by their feelings of marginality to facilitate social change and move an institution of society ever so slightly in a new direction. If the person can handle the feelings and conflicts inherent in marginality, then individual enhancement becomes a route to the advancement of the total social order.

Integration of Women

The critical factor in managing tokenism and marginality is numbers. Kanter's admonition that exaggerated effects follow the small token numbers is reinforced by Parkhurst's research population, which reported their greatest support came from members of their own countries or other foreign students. "These women offered such reasons as: we share the same background; they will help me when I need it; they understand my problems; our temperaments are the same; we can laugh at the same things" (Parkhurst 1982, p. 11). Seemingly, some of the negative impact of marginality can be mediated to the extent that there are other marginal persons with whom to share concerns. But the personal and professional strains cannot be eliminated. Women planning to enter careers, especially those traditionally dominated by males, can prepare for severe personal and professional challenges as well as rewarding growth and development throughout the years ahead.

4.4. Preparation at a United States Institution of Higher Learning for a Professional Role

Study in the United States presents special challenges to women from other countries. Upon arrival in a new culture, most people experience some amount of culture shock. Women in particular need to be aware of this phenomenon for they may encounter cultural norms and expectations for women that differ widely from those in their home countries. A person often interprets and perhaps misinterprets phenomena in the new culture in terms of the home culture. It will take time to learn the rules and norms in the new setting, especially those relating to gender.

Women have been striving for equality at U.S. institutions of higher education for many years. The results of these efforts still may not be clearly evident. For example, there may be few female professors in some fields of study or few females in high-level administrative positions to serve as role models for the female student from another country. In some countries, female professionals may experience very equal working conditions; in others, they may experience subordinate conditions or professional positions may be unavailable to women. The point is that female students can expect to observe both similarities and differences in comparing women's roles in the United States and in the home countries. Recognition of this phenomena will help to lessen some of the initial cultural shock when students find there are few women in leadership positions with whom they can communicate.

Orientation sessions on campuses planned especially for students from other countries can be helpful to the new student. Information distributed at these sessions can help participants become acquainted with the university and community and with a variety of services available to students from other countries.

4.4.1. Balancing the personal-familial and student roles

In an earlier section of this chapter, personal and familial roles and responsibilities were discussed. When these roles are combined with the student or professional preparation role, the balance between the roles needs to be carefully examined. This may be of particular concern to women with family responsibilities who arrive in the United States to study. Chaney (1980, p. viii) states that women moving to strange cultures need help in "reconstituting their support networks and restructuring their households." They are in need of assistance to ease the burdens of reestablishing their links to health, education, and community services, as well as to commercial establishments.

In many parts of the world work roles and family roles are very closely intertwined (Papanek 1977). In industrialized societies such as the United States, however, there may be some conflict between these roles. Success as a student may be influenced by resolution of such conflicts. For example, a woman who arrived recently from one of the African countries with her two-year-old son could not devote the time necessary to adequately learn about university procedures and adjust to her responsibilities as a student until acceptable child-care arrangements had been made. Making these arrangements was an entirely new responsibility for her. In her home country, she lived in an extended family and the child was cared for by members of the family. Once the arrangements were completed here, her concern and worry were alleviated, and she was able to devote time and thought to her role as a student.

Other aspects of a woman's familial role that may affect her professional preparation role include locating household goods and furnishings, learning to use and care for appliances, selecting shopping facilities, buying clothing for cold climates, learning about public transportation systems, locating laundry services, and locating community agencies that provide assistance and information to international students. The international offices on some campuses can assist in these areas by including the information in orientation materials or by maintaining a list of interested students, faculty, or community groups who volunteer to help international students adjust to the United States. Another source of assistance is other students from the home country who have experienced the adjustment period and culture shock themselves. Often, they are invaluable resources, and they can provide, for example, information on where to shop for ingredients needed to prepare foods eaten in the home country but not commonly available in the United States. They can also respond to referral questions, that is, whom to contact for what information.

Resolution of conflicts related to personal and family responsibilities frees a person to devote more time and thought to academic pursuits. Because many of these responsibilities are assumed by women in other cultures, it is particularly helpful to women who are involved in professional preparation to have information that will assist in lessening the strain of meeting those household responsibilities in the United States.

4.4.2. Responsibilities in the professional preparation process

In most cases, international graduate students arrive at the U.S. institution with definite professional goals. They have been accepted into programs of study and most likely have been assigned to advisers or persons who will work with them in identifying courses in which to enroll. In order to plan the best possible programs, it is essential that students from other countries communicate their professional goals and describe their work situations at home as clearly as possible to the advisers. When possible, it may be helpful to request an adviser who is familiar with the student's country or at least has had international work experience. Together, the adviser and student can identify those courses that meet the requirements and are also appropriate to achievement of the student's goals.

For female students, there may be additional hurdles not encountered by male students as frequently in program planning. First, future roles of women may be less clearly defined. The woman may be among the first group of women from the home country to be sent abroad for study. It may be expected that upon her return home she will serve as a role model for other women. She may also become involved at the planning and policy-making level and may shape overall policies to benefit women (Tinker 1981; Cook 1981). A program of study may not include preparation for these roles. The female student who thinks she will find herself in this type of situation in the future has the responsibility to communicate this to the adviser openly so that these needs may be addressed in her program of study. There is little flexibility in some programs; however, with careful early planning, it may be possible to include preparation for these future professional activities.

The importance of communication with one's adviser has been mentioned. Communication is frequently a second hurdle encountered by female students from other countries. In chapter 3, Michael Moravcsik discusses communication and its objectives. A student develops communication skills and patterns that will be essential to the professional role. Cultural norms, however, may interfere with how women from some countries communicate. They may not feel comfortable in expressing their ideas freely in academic settings. In their home countries, asking questions of a professor might be unacceptable. In the United States, however, students are expected to be critical thinkers. It is acceptable for female students to pose questions to other students and professors. Although it may be unacceptable in her home country for a woman to make an appointment with a male professor, it may be necessary at times in the United States.

Understanding the rules and practices of communication is critical. Students may need to observe other students carefully to learn these rules and to learn what can be asked of whom and when. One young female student from an Asian country made frequent appointments with her professors. At the appointments, however, she was always accompanied by her husband, who spoke to the professors for her. After several of these sessions, one professor finally asked the husband to leave so she could communicate directly with the woman. The woman nervously but competently carried out the conference on her own. She learned that she could communicate by herself and that, furthermore, as a student, she had the responsibility to do so.

Students studying at U.S. institutions have another responsibility, that of continuously adapting and applying newly gained knowledge and experiences to their home countries. These students are being professionally prepared in a culture other than their own and in a society that is highly technological. As they add to their education, they need to keep in mind the knowledge and learning systems indigenous to their own cultures (Brokenshaw, Warren, and Werner 1980) and to consider if, and how, what they are learning might be adapted and integrated into the existing systems at home.

A group of female international students meeting together in a course designed especially to assist them in adapting what they had learned in the United States to their home cultures expressed several such concerns. Some of these women indicated that they would be working at the village level. Translation of what they had learned in English to their native dialect was a concern. Because they had no words that would convey the same meanings, conceptual understandings were identified as important so that ideas could be accurately translated. Another concern was that they had used very elaborate and up-to-date equipment in the United States, equipment that would not be available in their work at home. Many of the women indicated that upon their return they would be in situations in which they would develop programs for other women. They stressed the importance of staying in touch with what was happening at home. They needed to remain aware of the roles and situation of women at home while studying in the United States in order to be helpful in the development of programs for women.

While studying in the United States, students may want to relate as much of their education as possible to their home countries. They should take advantage of opportunities provided by professors who encourage application of content to the situation in the home country as part of course assignments. This type of adaptation and application assumes that students will continue to be informed and knowledgeable about events in their home countries through regular reading of newspapers and correspondence with informed individuals. Upon return home students can then more easily

Integration of Women

adapt academic experiences to suit the local circumstances (Altbach 1982).

Doyle (1980) states that, when possible, it is an excellent idea for students to conduct research in their own countries on problems that are pertinent and important to the home culture. Women who do this could use this research in their future professional roles by building on it. Having established some credibility in an area would be especially helpful to women who will return home to work. They may be among the first women in professional positions with research experience. At a conference on women and development held at Wellesley College, Awe (1977, p. 315) supported this idea by saying that "the time has now come when emphasis should be on indigenous scholars; by virtue of their permanent membership in their society they are likely to have a better insight into its problems and the areas that need closest attention. Because of the present position of women in developing countries, research on women must also be policy oriented, but initiated by local scholars who can best indicate priorities."

Women who return home and are professionally involved may indeed be in situations where they can develop programs for women. They may, however, benefit by learning new ways for introducing ideas or for informing women directly rather than relying on indirect means, in which information does not necessarily pass freely. The dissemination points for information may be traditional male gathering places or community meetings attended by men (Chaney, Simmons, and Staudt 1979). Information reaches women in these cases only when men communicate within the household the information they have learned. This is what Cloud (1979) refers to as the "Trickle-Over-Theory." Female students may gain ideas about direct information dissemination through participation in special educational opportunities while in the United States. These may be special professional short courses offered on or off campus for women interested in gaining specific expertise, such as management skills. They may also offer ideas on developing a network system whereby women could be informed of educational opportunities.

Women who attended the NGO Forum or Alternative Women's Conference held in Copenhagen in 1980 frequently spoke of the responsibilities they felt for transferring to others the knowledge and skills they had acquired. They urged the establishment of international networks among women (Office of Women in Development 1980). The chapter on alumni networking and an earlier section of this chapter should be of some assistance in increasing understanding of a network system. Participation in women's activities while a student at a U.S. institution can provide an opportunity for actually becoming a part of a network. Groups such as women in development, women in science, or women in education exist on many campuses. The people involved can be the beginning of a student's own professional network for sharing similar concerns. The acquaintances made can be invaluable contacts in future endeavors.

Attending and participating in campus activities may be beneficial in other ways. These activities provide opportunities for interaction with other people, who may include U.S. students, international students, faculty members, or interested members of the community. Through interactions with others, friendships may be formed. These friendships may be very important when moments of loneliness or anxiety are experienced, as discussed earlier in this chapter.

4.4.3. Using professional and community involvement opportunities to enhance professional development

One's professional development can be enhanced through participation in professional and community activities. There may be opportunities to share information about the home culture at these activities. Having the opportunity to prepare and deliver a presentation and to respond to and ask questions assists in developing confidence, as well as helping future professionals gain some skills that will become important to them in their professional involvements. These same activities may also highlight differences between the student and local community members, thus giving the notion of marginality immediate reality.

Not all programs of study in the United States provide on-the-job experiences such as practicums or internships. Involvement in professional organizations at the local, state, and national levels brings students in contact with practicing professionals. Students can discuss with these individuals their professional roles and responsibilities. Perhaps these interactions will lead to the opportunity to actually spend time with the professionals in on-site visits. Such opportunities would be of special importance to the woman who may have had limited professional opportunities in her own country and limited opportunities for interaction with other professionals.

Becoming acquainted with community members and organizations, through visits with families and through sharing information about life at home with elementary and secondary school students and members of various community groups, can be invaluable in the student's professional preparation. All the individuals involved gain better understanding of one another and of how to communicate clearly. The international student gains a clearer picture of the United States and U.S. citizens gain a more accurate understanding of life in another culture. People learn from one another. Women learn that there are positive aspects to the roles of women in cultures other than their own, and that there are positive aspects of their roles from which women in other cultures can learn. Moreover, shared cultural values become apparent.

Taking the opportunity to learn about the community and services available could also make a positive contribution to the student's professional development. There are many resources in most communities of which she can take advantage.

As stated earlier, a professional environment can be bounded or described in many ways, and each individual is influenced by many other people, groups, and structures. So it is during the professional preparation period. Students can describe the environment as the departments in which they are studying or expand it to include the whole university, professional associations, and the community. The more exposure students have to other peoples and groups in the United States, the more experiences they will have as resources to contribute, as appropriate, to their professional roles in the home countries.

We have pointed out that students from other countries who prepare at U.S. institutions to become professionals may have experienced culture shock upon their arrival in U.S. communities. They need to expect and prepare for reentry or reverse culture shock upon return to their home countries (Warren and Patten 1981). In fact, the reverse culture shock may be greater than the initial culture shock. Brislin and Van Buren (1974) report that those individuals who most successfully adapt to a new culture may be the least successful at readjusting upon return to their home countries.

Increased education is beneficial but it can also be an obstacle for women returning to their home cultures. Smith (1980), reporting on interviews with fifteen women representing ten countries, describes their perceptions of the cultural adaptation process and their comparisons of family life in the United States and their home countries. Many of these women were from countries where women's roles are quite different from the roles of women in the United States. The women had become accustomed to the freedoms and independence experienced by women in the United States, and they were adapting to a different pattern of living. The researcher concludes that these women will experience difficulties and reverse culture shock upon return to their home countries.

Reverse culture shock can be lessened, however, if a person is prepared. As a woman professional begins to be integrated into her new role, she may need to look closely at how she has changed. She may have adjusted, for example, to speaking openly to men and to being free to make personal decisions for herself. Thus, it may take some time for the woman to readjust and to work out acceptable new modes of operation.

4.5. Conclusion

Women have always made significant and essential contributions to society. Some have been recognized internationally, whereas others are not nearly so well known. What is especially exciting is that an increasingly wide range of opportunities is becoming available to women. There are female engineers, trade union leaders, and politicians as well as doctors, professors, and social workers. Furthermore, it is no longer impossible to identify female role models. There are examples of women planners, administrators, policy makers, construction workers, and scholars.

Women who have achieved professional positions have served to make it easier for subsequent generations of professional women. They have blazed new trails, identified and overcome barriers, succeeded where other women have never been leaders before, and provided ample evidence that gender and competence are not predictably linked.

Those who are preparing or "retooling" for a professional life are facing both difficult responsibilities and exciting challenges. Despite the significant increase in the number of professional women, they remain, for the most part, in the minority when compared with numbers of male colleagues. Thus, women entering professional positions will have to consider building networks, balancing responsibilities, dealing with tokenism, and adjusting to marginality. These women, too, will be role models and may, because they are female, have to "prove" their competence. They must acknowledge that they may be examples, whether they wish to be or not. These responsibilities are not necessarily negative, however. They present challenges which, if faced carefully and creatively, offer women opportunities to make significant changes in their societies. The present is molded, in part, by the past. As a woman prepares for a professional position, she may wish to remember that the past is something to be used and that, as Ping Hsing of Taiwan writes,

> But in the warp and woof of time
> Is already woven
> The silk of the present   (Ping 1978)

Today, professional women can look back and learn from the experiences of the courageous women who preceded them, take advantage of the multitude of new opportunities now available, and contribute to building a base for a future in which all members of society are encouraged to make the best possible contributions to their societies.

References Cited

Altbach, Philip G. 1982. Higher education in advanced developing countries. *Prospects* 12:293–310.

Awe, Bolanle. 1977. Reflections on the Conference on Women and Development: I. In *Women and national development: The complexities of change.* Edited by the Wellesley Editorial Committee. Chicago: The University of Chicago Press.

Boakari, Francis Musa. 1982. Foreign student reentry: The case of 'the hurrying man.' *NAFSA Newsletter* 34(2):33, 39, 45–49.

Brislin, R., and H. Van Buren. 1974. Can they go home again? *International Educational and Cultural Exchange* 9(4)19–24.

Brokenshaw, David, D.M. Warren, and Oswald Werner. 1980. *Indigenous knowledge systems and development.* Washington, D.C.: University Press of America.

Castile, G.P., and G. Kushner, eds. 1981. *Persistent peoples.* Tucson: University of Arizona Press.

Chaney, Elsa M. 1980. *Women in international migration.* AID/OTR-147-80-46. Washington, D.C.: Office of Women in Development.

Chaney, Elsa, Emmy Simmons, and Kathleen Staudt. 1979. *Women in development.* Background paper for U.S. delegation to World Conference on Agrarian Reform and Rural Development, July.

Cloud, Kathleen. 1979. *The integration of women in agricultural development.* Paper presented at the meeting of the National Association of State Universities and Land Grant Colleges.

Cook, Gayla. 1981. Working with African women: Options for the West. *Africa Report* 26(2):43–46.

Doyle, Margaret. 1980. Response to agricultural extension education and the emergence of development woman. In *Home economics and agriculture in third world countries.* Edited by Miriam Seltzer. Proceedings of a seminar, University of Minnesota, May 14, 16, 23.

Global Networks. 1982. *The Christian Science Monitor,* 7 October, pp. B1-B5.

Information for development. 1982. *The NFE Exchange* (21):1-8.

Kanter, Rosabeth Moss. 1977. Some effects of proportions on group life: Skewed sex ratios and responses to token women. *American Journal of Sociology* (82):965-990.

Moone, J.R. 1981. Persistence with change: A property of sociocultural dynamics. In *Persisent Peoples.* Edited by G.P. Castile and G. Kushner. Tucson: University of Arizona Press.

Office of Women in Development. 1980. *Women in development.* Report to the Committee on Foreign Relations, United States Senate, and the Committee on Foreign Affairs, United States House of Representatives. Washington, D.C.: Agency for International Development.

Papanek, Hanna. 1977. Development Planning for Women. In *Women and National Development: The Complexities of Change.* Edited by Wellesley Editorial Committee. Chicago: The University of Chicago Press.

Parkhurst, Marilyn. 1982. A study of selected foreign women's perceptions of their professional education and training in the United States. Unpublished manuscript. Michigan State University.

Ping, Hsing. 1978. Voices of women: An Asian anthology. Delhi: Asian Church Women's Conference.

Shack, W.A., and E.P. Skinner, eds. 1979. *Strangers in African societies.* Berkeley: University of California Press.

Simmel, G. 1921. Introduction to the science of society. Translated by R.E. Park and E.W. Burgess. Chicago: University of Chicago Press. Originally published in 1908 as *Soziologie.* Leipzig: Duncker and Humblot.

Smith, Betty Jo. 1980. Women in development in Latin America. In *The Role of Women in International Agriculture and Food Development.* Edited by Barbara Chesser and Norman E. Tooker. Proceedings of a conference, University of Nebraska, Lincoln, January 30-31.

Stonequist, E.V. 1961. *The marginal man: A study in personality and culture conflict.* New York: Russell and Russell, Inc.

The Stranger. In *The sociology of Georg Simmel.* Translated and edited by K.H. Wolff. New York: Free Press.

Tinker, Irene. 1981. Policy strategies for women in the 1980's. *Africa Report* 26(2):11-16.

TRANET: Transnational Network of Appropriate Alternative Technologies. 1982. Rangely, Maine: Transnational Network.

Warren, D.M., and Sonia Patten. 1981. Cross-cultural interactions: The transition and reentry processes. *Anthropology and Humanism Quarterly* (6):20-24.

The Women and Food Information Network Newsletter. 1982. Tucson, Arizona: Women and Food Information Network.

Bibliography

Axinn, Nancy. 1981. Inappropriate technology transferred or biscuits be damned. In *Responding to the needs of rural women*. Edited by Eloise Murray. Proceedings of a conference sponsored by the Center for Women in Development, The South-East Consortium for International Development, and the United States Department of Agriculture at Kentucky State University, Frankfort, May 4-5.

Boserup, Ester. 1970. *Woman's role in economic development*. New York: St. Martin's Press.

Derryck, Vivian Lowery. 1979. *The comparative functionality of formal and non-formal education for women: Final report* AID/OTR-147-78-14. Washington, D.C.: Office of Women in Development, Agency for International Development.

Grygill, Carolyn E. 1982. The role of the natural resource professional in her native country. In *Women in natural resources: An international perspective*. Edited by Molly Stock, Jo Ellen Force, and Dixie Ehrenreich. Proceedings of a conference, University of Idaho, Moscow, March 8-9.

Leacock, Eleanore. 1977. Reflections on the conference on women and development: III. In *Women and national development: The complexities of change*. Edited by Wellesley Editorial Committee. Chicago: The University of Chicago Press.

Mazumdar, Vina. 1977. Reflections on the conference on women and development: IV. In *Women and national development: The complexities of change*. Edited by Wellesley Editorial Committee. Chicago: The University of Chicago Press.

Mickelson, Kaye Via. 1982. Networking...mentoring—neither happen magically! In *Women in natural resources: An international perspective*. Edited by Molly Stock, Jo Ellen Force, and Dixie Ehrenreich. Proceedings of a conference, University of Idaho, Moscow, March 8-9.

You will be courteous to your elders who have explored to the point from which you may advance; and helpful to your juniors who will progress farther by reason of your labors.... Your aim will be knowledge and wisdom, not the reflected glamour of fame.... You will not accept credit that is due another, or harbor jealousy of an explorer who is more fortunate.

—*The Society of Fellows, Harvard*

5.

Research and Publication

Motoko Y. Lee
D. Y. Lee

5.1. Introduction

This chapter is written primarily for those students from developing countries who are now studying in the United States and will return to their home countries to function as scientists. It is intended to explain to them, while they are in the United States, the conduct of research and the publication of research results. It is also intended to be useful to those who will become administrators of research institutes or laboratories in their home countries upon completion of study in the United States.

We hope the student will expose himself to the materials, facilities, and training recommended in this chapter *before* he leaves for his home country. With such exposure, we hope he will be better prepared not only to engage in research and publication, but also become a leader of the professional community of his country in its future development.

Many of the suggested materials and facilities may not be available at the present time in the institution or organization where the student will be returning to work. That does not mean his knowledge about such materials and facilities will be useless. On the contrary, the returned student will make use of it (1) through collaboration with U.S. scientists with whom he established contact before returning to his country, (2) by incorporating his knowledge in guiding the future direction of his country's research and publication activities, and (3), most important, by adapting his knowledge to the particular work environment to which he will be returning. This adaptation is one of the great challenges the returned student faces, since he knows more about his future work environment than anyone else, and thus, he will have to guide himself in making this adaptation.

This chapter is not intended to be a comprehensive "how to" guide for conducting research and writing scholarly papers, since extensive references on these subjects are already available. We will, rather, place a greater emphasis on identifying reference materials and relevant facilities that will be useful to the student in his future research and publishing endeavors.

This chapter is written with two basic premises: First, we believe publishing is an integral and necessary part of research. Second, we believe that science and scientific research have no national boundaries. While we recognize the variation in availability of certain facilities, funds, and other resources, the basic principles of science and research are universal.

5.2. Need for Research and Publication in Developing Countries

Scientific research in developing countries and publication of the results are needed for three major reasons. First, research results in one country may not be applicable to another country, depending on the subject matter. Some subjects, such as plant or animal breeding and many areas of agricultural research, are environmentally specific. Other subjects are socioculturally specific. A proper strategy for implementing an education program in a rural community is an example of a socioculturally specific subject. With the exception of some fields such as mathematics and physics, the returned student may find that much of what he learned in the United States needs to be questioned and examined as to its applicability to his own country. He will need to conduct research in order to determine whether the research findings generated in the United States are indeed universal and can be used in solving his country's problems, or whether modifications are needed for them to be applied in his country.

Second, among developed countries, to a certain extent, research findings have been exchanged to enhance knowledge, but the scientific data bases in many fields will not be complete unless findings from developing countries can also be incorporated. To that end, the returned student can make a significant contribution in conducting research and in making the results available through publications to scientists in other parts of the world.

Third, in view of the long history of colonialism experienced in many developing countries, the single most important long-term objective of these countries is to improve living conditions and to reduce dependency on technologically advanced countries. Without research and subsequent innovations, such dependency will be perpetuated.

5.3. Research

The first step in research is to find interesting, significant, and relevant problems or topics. In some cases, especially if the returned student is working for a government agency, the research topic may be a specific problem assigned by a superior. Even if the returned student already has research topics, it is important to be sure that someone else has not solved the problems, or to know what has been done with a particular problem or related problems. To answer those questions, the researcher needs to conduct a thorough literature search, so as to avoid "reinventing the wheel." After research topics or subtopics have been decided on, the next step is to convince the government, foundations, or other funding agencies to fund the research project. In general, convincing the home government agency requires that a research topic have a problem-solving orientation. In any case, a research proposal will have to be written. Once the funds necessary to carry out the research are available, the research must be conducted in a scientific and cost-effective manner. After the data have been gathered, the meaning, significance, and implications must be extracted from the data. In all of this, certain basic tools for research design and data analysis are required. In the following sections, we will highlight the key elements of and provide useful references on literature search, proposal writing, research design, and data analysis.

Those who want to start a research group or, sooner or later, become research managers (scientists as administrators) need to know something about research management. For this, we recommend the small book *Development and management of research groups* by Robert V. Smith (1980). It deals with topics such as obtaining grant support, recruiting research personnel, purchasing equipment, writing reports, and maintaining literature files. Although it is a guide for university researchers, it is also useful for any individual involved in research management.

Another brief book, both useful and enjoyable, is *Advice to a young scientist* by Nobel Laureate P. B. Medawar (1979). It deals with many subjects, including how to choose a research topic, how to get along with collaborators and administrators, and how to write and present a scientific paper. We recommend it to anyone engaged in scientific research anywhere in the world.

5.3.1. Literature search

The first step in any research process is a literature search. The purposes of a literature search are (1) to become familiar with past studies about the topic to learn what is already known, even in new areas of inquiry; (2) to obtain information about closely related studies; (3) to develop a theoretical understanding of the chosen topic; and (4) to become familiar with methods and instruments used in past studies on the topics or related topics.

There are a number of ways to conduct a literature search in college and university libraries in the United States. One may begin (1) in the card catalog, (2) in periodical indexes and abstracts, (3) with a computer search service through the batch system, and (4) with interactive (on-line) computer search services. A librarian should be consulted about the availability and the cost of the third and fourth approaches. Generally, these means are available in most libraries in U.S. universities and large colleges. However, computer search services may not be available in many developing countries. Thus, we urge students who are still in the United States to inquire at their school libraries as to the availability of these literature search services for overseas clientele. (For example, Iowa State University's library will conduct computer literature searches for a home country library or for a scholar, provided that the home country institution or organization will bear the cost of the search and postage. It also provides interlibrary loan services to overseas libraries.)

To begin a literature search using any of the four approaches, one should first compile a list of descriptors, the key words used in looking for references. A librarian may be consulted to determine whether a thesaurus (a list of descriptors) is available for a particular subject area, and the librarian can also assist in compiling descriptors. A careful and parsimonious selection of descriptors is crucial, especially in a computer literature search, in order to minimize expenses and obtain the maximum results. The following sections describe the different approaches to a literature search.

5.3.1.1. Card catalog

Generally, research begins with the card (or filmed) catalog in the library. The card catalog lists books by authors, titles, and subjects. Even books that are closely related to the chosen topic may include references to the topic. Using the list of compiled descriptors, the researcher should check through the indexes of books. Books may be major sources for the theoretical framework of research, and they will often lead to other sources on the topic which, in turn, reveal more references. This approach is adequate for a preliminary study of references, but the researcher cannot assume that everything has been covered.

5.3.1.2. Periodical indexes and abstract publications

Periodical indexes and periodical abstract publications list publications in a number of periodicals with the names of authors, the titles, and

Research and Publication

publishers. Additionally, periodical abstract publications include a short abstract for each listed publication. Faculty members or librarians can assist in identifying indexes and abstract publications in a particular field. Here again, a list of descriptors is necessary to search through an index or abstract.

The following major indexes and abstract publications are likely to be found in most university and college libraries:

- periodical indexes—

    Current Index to Journals in Education
    Education Index
    Engineering Index
    Government Reports Index
    Index Medicus
    Research in Education
    Science Citation Index
    Social Sciences Citation Index

- periodical abstracts—

    Abstracts in Anthropology
    Biological Abstracts
    Chemical Abstracts
    Dissertation Abstracts International
    Physics Abstracts
    Psychological Abstracts
    Sociological Abstracts

University Microfilms may also be a good source for abstracts.

If a journal article listed in an index or an abstract publication cannot be located in the library, the librarian can assist in arranging an interlibrary loan from another library. Most U.S. libraries will honor similar requests from libraries overseas.

5.3.1.3. Computer search service

Many university and college libraries provide computer search services for periodical materials. The cost of a computer literature search depends on the number of indexes and abstract publications (databases) and the number of articles compiled in a list. In general, a compiled search requires that one consult with a librarian. Before consulting a librarian, the researcher must have a clear idea as to what types of information he is looking for in periodicals and a tentative list of descriptors, which will be modified with the help of the librarian for the purpose of the computer literature search. The researcher should also decide on the period of time to be covered by the computer search. That is, should it cover from 1965 to the present or should it be limited to only the most recent articles in a database?

5.3.1.4. On-line computer search

An on-line computer search is an interactive computer search relatively new to most campuses. This approach is fast and efficient since the researcher receives the results in a matter of seconds, thus permitting modification of descriptors as he narrows his selection of periodicals. This type of search will also require the assistance of a librarian.

Database computer searches (on-line or batch) are often accompanied by a delivery system through which the full text of the cited paper or report can be provided to the user. Two comprehensive listings of databases are—

- Williams, M.E. 1982. *Computer-readable data bases: A directory and source book,* Washington, D.C.: American Society for Information Science. This contains the names and producers of more than 700 databases worldwide, totaling more than 80,000,000 references.
- Sanders, J.B. *Information market place.* Annual. European Association of Scientific Information Dissemination Centers. New York: R.R. Bowker Co.

Computer searches are available through most large university libraries. Additionally, a growing number of private information service firms specialize in computer search and document delivery systems, and university libraries often purchase services from them. Thus, a student might consider making some arrangements with his U.S. library before returning to the home country, so that he could request such a service in the future from overseas. (In some developing countries, libraries are already utilizing the computer literature search services provided by European libraries.) Or the student might consider dealing directly with computer search services by writing to them while in the United States. (In some foreign countries these services are already available.) Well-known computer search services include—

- BLAISE LINE/BLAISE-LINK (British Library Automated Information Service)
  Address: British Library, 2 Sheraton Street, London, U.K., WIL 4BH
  Telephone: (01) 636-1544

Research and Publication

- BRS (Bibliographic Retrieval Services)
  Address: Bibliographic Retrieval Services, Inc., 1462 Erie Blvd.,Schenectady, NY 12305, USA
  Telephone: (518) 374-5011

- DIALOG
  Address: 3460 Hillview Ave., Palo Alto, CA 94304, USA
  Telephone: (415) 585-3785

- ORBIT (On-line Retrieval of Bibliographic Information Time-shared)
  Address: SDC Search Service, System Development Corp., Colorado Ave., Santa Monica, CA 90406, USA
  Telephone: (213) 829-7511

A useful listing of information services, including key personnel, addresses, telephone numbers, rates, databases, and other information, can be found in *Directory of Fee-Based Information Services,* published by Information Alternative, Woodstock, New York 12498.

In addition to the published literature, one may wish to know what research activities are currently being undertaken with regard to the research topic. Such information can be obtained from, for example, Smithsonian Institutional Science Information Exchange (SISIE) by contacting Science Information Exchange, Inc., Room 300, Madison Bank Building, 1730 M Street, N.W., Washington, D.C. 20036.

The search process just described may seem a luxury upon returning home. However, even though the library at home may not have facilities of its own for computer searches, researchers may very well find that their institute or organization can afford to purchase computer search services through local libraries or by dealing directly with U.S. or European libraries.

5.3.2. Proposal writing

Proposal writing requires that one plan carefully all the steps of a project and make at least preliminary decisions, such as what is needed and when in order to carry out the entire project. Budgets cannot be proposed without making all those decisions, nor is the researcher able to communicate the significance of the proposed project to those who will be reading the proposal without having made some project decisions.

Before writing a proposal, the researcher should contact potential funding agencies or institutions to find out whether they would be interested in considering the project, and they should be provided with a brief description of the proposed project (preproposal). The researcher should also ask for the regulations and forms for the submission of project proposals and ought to follow the format and regulations for submitting a proposal. In some instances, guidance beyond that provided by the agency or sponsor may be needed. The following discussion is based mainly on *Research proposals: A guide for scientists, technologists and research institutes in developing countries,* published by the United Nations (1973), and on our own experiences in writing research proposals. We will discuss only the major points. For more detailed information, we recommend the United Nations book. (This book was written to provide guidance for research proposals on the problems of developing countries that are to be submitted to institutions in developed countries for funding. Yet, this guide will be helpful for any proposal writing, and it also includes a sample proposal.) The outline suggested here is by no means sacred. Appropriate adjustments in the format of a proposal may be required, depending on the topic and the funding agency's requirements. Our outline also covers points that one may want to consider when reviewing or evaluating proposals submitted by others.

5.3.2.1. Cover-title pages

The cover-title pages usually include the title of the proposal, the names of the authors (principal investigators), their affiliations, the name and the address of the organization to which the proposal is to be submitted, and the date of submission. Depending on the regulations of the potential funding agency, the cover page may also include the amount of funding sought, the duration of the study, the proposal number, the endorsements (signatures) of relevant persons, including the appropriate administrator of the researcher's institution.

5.3.2.2. Summary or abstract

If the proposal is long (more than ten pages), it is a good idea to provide a short summary stating concisely all the key points necessary to give the reviewers an overview of what is being proposed. This will be helpful to those who do not have time to read the entire proposal, yet who want to know about the proposal.

5.3.2.3. Table of contents

The United Nations' *Guide* recommends that a table of contents be included if the text has more than one level of subdivision or one level with more than five headings. The table of contents should include all the headings and page numbers.

5.3.2.4. Lists of tables and figures

Again, the United Nations' *Guide* recommends that a list of tables and a list of figures be included if more than five of any of these appear in the proposal.

5.3.2.5. Text of the proposal

The materials in a proposal need to be arranged in a way that will best communicate the researcher's ideas to the readers (the reviewers) and impress them with the value of the proposed study. A task group appointed by the United Nations reviewed the document preparation manuals of several leading research organizations and adopted an outline that appears in the *Guide* (p. 7). We have modified this outline somewhat to make it more universally applicable.

Introduction. The introduction should briefly present the problem that is to be studied, the reasons why the study is important, and the scope and the major objective of the study. The information should be presented in an explicit manner so that even those who are in another field will be interested in learning more about the project by reading the rest of the proposal.

Background. The researcher cannot assume that the problem to be investigated is familiar to those who will evaluate the proposal. For this reason, the background section should provide more than general information about the country, and it should include—

- the current situation or the current practices, and a description of past attempts to solve the problem;
- a description of past studies related to this problem, conducted at home and abroad;
- the potential effects of the project, upon its successful completion, on the immediate target group of subjects, and the broader socioeconomic, sociopolitical, and other ramifications of the project.

Techno-economic justification (optional). If a techno-economic justification is included, its purpose is to convince the reviewer that the proposed project has a sound economic basis and that the anticipated (hypothesized) solution will be economically feasible. The technical discussion should include possible alternative solutions that are technically feasible, and it should provide a rationale for the optimum alternatives in both technical and economic terms.

If the solution is entirely pending on the results of the proposed study, then this section is not needed. The economic justification of the exploratory study can be incorporated in the background discussion, but this section is important when one is seeking funds from a source outside his country.

5.3.2.6. Methods and procedure

In the methods and procedure section, the research design is presented. The researcher should state what work will be done, in what order, and with what method and instrumentation; he should also state what data will be collected and how they will be analyzed. Sections 5.3.3 and 5.3.4 of this chapter discuss research design and data analysis.

5.3.2.7. Work schedule

A timetable or work schedule for the research project must be included. A chart format is highly recommended, since it will be easier for the reviewer to see and, later, for the researcher to use in determining whether he is following his schedule. A sample work schedule is given in appendix A. In order to develop such a chart, the work must be divided into tasks, and each task must be clearly defined. The chart should also indicate the submission time of the report (and progress reports, if required).

5.3.2.8. Management of projects

A presentation of the division of tasks among the members of the research team should be included. Each person's role needs to be clearly defined in terms of task assignments. If any part of the project needs to be conducted away from the base institution, the reason why that part of work cannot be conducted there must be given. The vitas for members of the research team should be included as an appendix to the proposal.

5.3.2.9. Budget

The budget for the project should be prepared on a separate sheet (or as a separate document, depending on the regulations of the sponsoring agency). A researcher is accountable for spending every part of the funds, so all the possible expenses should be included in the budget proposal. Some funding agencies will not allow any deviations in spending from the original proposal. In other words, it may not be possible to shift fund allocation from one item to another at will. The researcher is making a budget for the coming year or for some time in the future. Therefore, it is important to take into account inflation factors and salary increases in the budget. If the researcher is not certain about the estimated costs, it is advisable to include the larger figures of any estimations. It is possible to negotiate a budget with a potential funding agency, if that agency is seriously interested in funding the project.

The designated office in charge of contracts and grants at an institution should be consulted about the budget, since that office is aware of the various regulations related to receiving research funds from outside sources.

Research and Publication

The following is a sample list of items frequently found in a budget proposal:
- personnel
    - —salaries and wages
    - —fringe benefits
    - —consultant and contract services
- permanent equipment
- expendable supplies
- travel expenses
- publication costs
- computer time
- other
- total direct cost (sum of the above)
- total indirect cost (overhead)
- total project cost

In this listing, indirect costs are defined by an established formula agreed upon by the funding agency and the institution where the research is carried out. This listing, of course, should be modified to suit the needs of a particular project.

5.3.2.10. Qualifications of the professional staff and institution

The research proposal should include a description of the institution where the research will be done. The capabilities and facilities of the institution should be highlighted with regard to the field of the proposed project. A brief description of technically related projects that were undertaken or are currently taking place in the institution should be included, as well as biographical sketches of key personnel in the appropriate field at the institution. Such information will convince the potential funding agency that (1) the institution or department is properly equipped to conduct a research project (or to receive new equipment, if that is what is being proposed) and that (2) the institution has a good record in conducting studies with qualified researchers. The young professional who has recently graduated from a U.S. university should state that fact and provide information as to his previous training, that is, where and with whom it was received, and what facilities he has previously worked with. It may be appropriate for the young professional to ask some of those persons under whom he did his previous work to assist as consultants to the project. Having a well-established consultant in a project will enhance the value of the proposal in the eyes of the reviewers, and, in fact, the consultant can be very helpful in carrying out the project.

5.3.2.11. Appendixes

Appendixes may be needed to provide the following information:

- vitas of the research team members, including that of the consultant, if any;
- relevant technical formulas or mathematical derivations referred to in the proposal;
- a list of abbreviations, if more than five abbreviations appear throughout the proposal; and
- data from preliminary study, if any have been compiled.

Proposals will be reviewed by experts in the field. In-house review will be done by someone in the funding agency, while peer review will be conducted by one or more scientists selected by the agency from among the experts in the particular field. Reviewers are usually given certain guidelines to follow. For example, reviewers selected by the National Science Foundation (NSF) examine proposals with regard to the following points:

- strengths and weaknesses in the approach and content
- originality and creativity of the proposed research
- past research record of the principal investigator(s) or other evidence of research potential to assess the likelihood for the principal investigator(s) to make an important and original contribution
- reasonableness of the budget requested
- appropriateness of the research environment, including equipment and other resources.

To locate funding sources, the following publications may be helpful. *Foundation Grants to Individuals,* 2nd edition (N.Y.: Foundation Center, 1979), has descriptions of grant programs for individuals (including individuals from other countries) offered by about 950 foundations. *Grants Register,* 7th edition (N.Y.: St. Martin's Press, 1980) lists more than 2,000 grant programs that are more international in scope. A sample page from the current edition of *Grants Register* is given in appendix B.

In addition to the guide published by the United Nations (1973), there are other similar publications, for example, *Grants: How to find out about them and what to do next,* by V.P. White (1975).

5.3.3. Research design

The purpose of research is to apply scientific methods to uncover regularities in the universe so that one can explain the occurrence of an event and predict it. The scientific method is a set of procedures and guidelines that make the investigation reliable and the conclusion valid. Blalock and Blalock (1982, p.8) summarize the steps in the scientific method as follows:

- the statement of the research problem or issue to be investigated, or the theoretical explanation to be tested;
- the translation of the abstract ideas in this theoretical explanation into concrete, explicitly identifiable ideas;
- the development of measures of the important variables in the theoretical explanation;
- the development of a research design to guide the inquiry into the research problem, so that the information gathered truly tests the validity of the explanation to the fullest extent possible;
- the selection of a set of methods that implement this design;
- the collection of research data;
- the analysis of this information in the context of the proposed explanation; and
- the interpretation of the information, or integration of the findings of the research with the existing knowledge base.

Through the literature search, the researcher becomes familiar with the theoretical perspectives and knowledge gained from past studies on the chosen subject, unless the subject is entirely new. The second step is to formulate hypotheses based on the literature, which will be tested in the research process, and to determine operationally defined measures (empirical measures) of the concepts in the hypotheses, before designing the study.

A research design is a total plan of research that should include decisions as to the unit of observation (and the unit of analysis, if different from the unit of observation), the time dimension of the study (longitudinal or one point in time), the scope of the study in terms of the target population to be studied, the scope of the study in terms of matters to be investigated (which will be mostly determined by the hypotheses selected), the method of data collection, the method of sample selection, and the data analysis plan. If hypotheses cannot be developed because of the newness of the subject matter, the researcher can attempt to conduct an exploratory study rather than a study to test certain hypotheses.

We will pay special attention to the methods of data collection (or the methods of observation) in the remainder of this section. The four most widely used methods of data collection are the experiment, survey, field study, and unobtrusive study.

5.3.3.1. Experiment

The experiment is the most rigorous approach in the scientific method. In an experiment, attributes of selected variables (called the independent variables) are manipulated to determine their effects on the target variables (called the dependent variables) under conditions where there is control for other variables or where their effects are kept constant. This method enables the researcher to determine the probable causal relationships between the dependent variables and the independent variables.

The underlying principle of the experimental method is the ideal. The researcher generally tries to approach the ideal by using multiple methods for proper sampling, or statistical control of certain variables, or both. A laboratory experiment provides the best advantage in manipulating some variables and controlling others. This is the most widely used method in the physical sciences.

In the social sciences, some laboratory experiments are used in areas such as experimental psychology. However, experiments in natural settings (quasi experiments) have gained popularity in recent years because of the increasing interest in evaluation research, the purpose of which is to evaluate the effectiveness of a program, for example, a teaching technique for elementary school pupils. In an experiment in a natural setting, one can hold constant the variables that are presumed to be noncausal by an appropriate selection of the sample characteristics (for example, age and sex), while manipulating the attributes of the independent variables by appropriate assignment of the sample subjects to the experimental group (those to receive the treatment) and to the control group (those not to receive the treatment). This type of experiment can be used to evaluate the effectiveness of developmental projects in developing countries.

The book by Blalock and Blalock (1982), mentioned earlier, has an excellent and concise chapter on experiments. The authors introduce basic concepts in experiments, including randomization of uncontrolled variables, interaction effects, and the effects of premeasurement. A more extensive discussion of the experimental method is found in *Experimental and quasi-experimental designs for research,* by Donald Campbell and Julian Stanley (1963). For techniques in evaluation research for which experiments in natural settings are typically used, we recommend *Evaluation: A systematic approach,* by Peter Rossi and Howard Freeman (1982), and *Handbook in research and evaluation,* by Stephen Isaac and William Michael (1981).

5.3.3.2. Sample survey

When the target of research is a large population of subjects, a sample survey is the appropriate design, unless the population is homogeneous. This is a widely used method in the social sciences, since the human population is highly heterogeneous with regard to almost any variable of in-

Research and Publication

terest to social scientists. The ultimate goal of a sample survey is to arrive at findings that can be generalized for the entire population, based on the data obtained from a sample of that population. There are three important considerations in conducting a sample survey: (1) obtaining a sample that will represent the population, (2) obtaining the data from the sample, and (3) making inferences about the population based on the data obtained from the sample.

The first consideration is sampling. Various sampling techniques are discussed in most research methods books (e.g., Babbie, 1983, and Bailey, 1978). A more technical discussion on sampling is found in *Survey sampling,* by Leslie Kish (1965).

The second consideration is the data collection procedure. The most commonly used procedures are (1) mailing a questionnaire to the sample population, (2) interviewing each subject in person, (3) interviewing each subject on the telephone, and (4) having subjects fill out a questionnaire as a group in the researcher's presence. The advantages and disadvantages of these procedures of data collection are discussed extensively in research methods books for the social sciences (e.g., Babbie 1983, Bailey 1978).

The third consideration is making inferences based on statistical analysis of the data. If data are gathered from a sample rather than from the total population, statistical methods are used to make inferences about the population, that is, to estimate the population characteristics based on the characteristics of the sample. Before he returns home, the student should take basic courses in statistics, if he anticipates that his future work may require statistics for sample surveys (and also for experiments with samples). Further discussion of data analysis is provided in the following section of this chapter.

During the design stage of the study, the researcher must make plans as to the types of statistical analyses to be used to test hypotheses. The researcher also needs to decide in what form the collected data ought to be, in order to use certain statistical tests. These decisions, if made in advance, will determine what questions are to be asked and in what way the answers should be collected, for example using the categorical or continuum method. These decisions are necessary to construct a questionnaire or an interview schedule and to decide on the data collection procedure. One caution about the survey method is that, with the exception of face-to-face interviews, this method assumes literacy (both in reading and writing) among the target subjects. Thus, in a developing country, the researcher may not be able to use mailed questionnaires with certain sectors of the population because of illiteracy among the subjects. Also, telephone interviews may be inappropriate because of the lack of a telephone in many households. A group interview may assume literacy, but the presence of the interviewer will alleviate some of the problems.

5.3.3.3. Field studies

Types of field studies range from participant observation, in which the researcher takes a part in the activities of the subjects, to nonparticipant observation, in which the researcher is an outside observer, confined to observing activities and asking questions of the subjects.

Conducting a field study in a sample of many communities, for example, will be impractical or impossible. Field study is generally chosen when the intention is (1) to explore the target subject (e.g., a community or an organization) without having any previous knowledge of it, (2) to study the target subject in depth, and (3) to approach a target subject unapproachable by any other method.

One of the difficulties with field study is the lack of standardization of data. Data obtained in a field study lack generalizability and are difficult to replicate. In general, field studies provide initial insights about the subjects, functioning as exploratory studies, and contribute to the future development of more structured studies in which hypothesis testing can be conducted with standardized data.

Tips for conducting successful field studies are available in almost any research method book. Two books written specifically about this method are *Participant observation* (1980) and *The ethnographic interview* (1979), both by James Spradley. Another book, which describes various experiences with the field study method, is *Field work experience: Qualitative approaches to social research,* by William Shaffir, Robert Stebbins, and Allan Turowetz (1980).

The field study method can be used in an area where the literacy rate is low. The main challenge is for the researcher to develop interpersonal skills in order to obtain the trust of his subjects and, at the same time, to prevent personal bias or attachment to the subjects from distorting his observations.

5.3.3.4. Unobtrusive studies

Unobtrusive studies include a wide range of approaches known by other names. They all have one thing in common: The presence of an observer or observational activities does not have an effect on the subjects. An unobtrusive study can be combined with an experiment, if the subjects are not aware that they are in an experiment or are being observed. The use of existing data collected by someone else is also unobtrusive, as is the content analysis of existing art forms such as literature and songs. Further information about content analysis is provided in *Content analysis for the social sciences and humanities* by Ole Holsti (1969). For use of historical data, *Theoretical methods in social history,* by Arthur Stinchcombe (1978), is available. Before starting a study, the researcher should consider use of existing data or documents as a viable alternative, especially if research facilities or funds are lacking. In some countries, data may be unavailable or unreliable. Therefore, it may be best to use a combination of methods, that is, data collection and use of data collected previously by others.

5.3.3.5. Errors in data collection

Before the data collection is begun, regardless of the method chosen, it is critical to minimize the possibility of errors in the data by a careful selection of the instruments of measurement (e.g., scale or questions). There are two types of errors that might be found in the data; one type is due to the unreliability of data, and the other is due to the questionable validity of the instruments chosen (Blalock and Blalock 1982). The former involves random errors in measurements. In other words, the person taking measurements is not obtaining correct readings from the instruments. This type of error makes the reliability of the data questionable. Random errors may occur because of the carelessness of the observer in observing or in reading the instruments, or in misunderstanding the respondent or even the data processing. These are not intended errors or systematically built-in errors. These errors in a variable are generally expected to be uncorrelated with all other variables, but they will weaken the correlations of the variable with other variables (Blalock and Blalock 1982). Multiple measurements of a variable will provide a safeguard against this type of error. It is also possible to correct the data for unreliability by using multiple measurements.

Nonrandom, or systematic, errors occur because of a built-in bias in the instrument or in the observer. This type of error raises a serious question as to the validity of the data, that is, whether the instrument is indeed a proper measure for the theoretical concept. Highly reliable measurements for a concept need not always be valid; for example, accurate readings may be taken from a wrong instrument. Great care must be taken in the selection of instruments so that they will provide valid measures of the concepts. Obtaining opinions from colleagues as to the validity of instruments will be helpful in minimizing validity problems. Through practice and logical thinking, the researcher can develop the capability of selecting valid operational measures for theoretical concepts. For a detailed discussion of reliability and validity and the differences between these two concepts, we suggest the handbook by Isaac and Michael (1981).

5.3.4. Data analysis

The following discussion will be limited to quantitative data analysis, since qualitative data depend on the ingenuity of each researcher for a meaningful presentation. That is to say, there are standardized methods for presenting qualitative data. We will emphasize the use of computers in the analysis of quantitative data. We believe it is important to become familiar with computer capabilities and the availability of statistical software.

Research and Publication

After data collection, the raw data need to be coded; that is, numerical values need to be assigned, if this has not been done already, and missing values should be assigned to the cases where certain data are missing. All of this should be done according to the conventions of the particular statistical software being used, before the data can be put into a computer.

There are three options for computer processing of the data: (1) the batch system using the main-frame computer, (2) the interactive terminal of the main-frame computer, and (3) the microcomputer. In the first option, the raw data are keypunched onto IBM cards and fed into the main-frame computer for analyses. In the second option, the raw data are fed directly from data sheets or questionnaires through the keyboard of the interactive terminal; the data are then sent to the main-frame computer from that terminal for analyses. In this option, it is also possible for the data to be put on IBM cards or on a magnetic tape or disk in the main-frame computer after being sent from the interactive terminal. The third option, which is becoming increasingly popular, involves feeding the data into a microcomputer, a self-contained unit.

The researcher must be certain that the appropriate statistical techniques are used to analyze the data for the purpose of description or for the purpose of hypothesis testing. A few basic statistics courses can provide reasonable familiarity with the most popularly used techniques.

There are a number of good books on statistics. For an elementary introduction to statistical methods, *Statistics: A tool for the social sciences,* by Lyman Ott, William Hendenhall, and Richard Lawson (1978) is recommended. For more advanced knowledge of statistical methods frequently used by researchers, *An introduction to statistical methods and data analysis,* by Ott (1977), is recommended for its clear, concise manner of presentation and the range of materials covered, which is wide enough for most users of statistics.

The researcher should not hesitate to seek advice from trained statisticians before making a final selection of statistical techniques in order to avoid misuse or abuse of statistics. Indeed, we strongly recommend obtaining advice prior to data collection instead of just before data analysis. A statistician can determine, before the researcher finalizes a data collection plan, whether the data to be collected with the chosen instruments will be the type of data that are suitable for the statistical techniques to be used in testing the hypotheses. Once data are collected, it may be too late to modify the form of the data to meet the researcher's assumptions.

There are a number of statistical software packages available for main-frame computers. SAS (Statistical Analysis System) and SPSS (Statistical Package for Social Sciences) are probably the most popular in the United States. Unfortunately, these software packages are very expensive. SPSS can be used with a wider variety of computers than SAS, which has been used, until recently, only with IBM computers. Both are extremely power-

Research and Publication

ful packages, and each individual must decide whether such packages, along with expensive main-frame computers, are needed for the types of data analysis and for the size of data he is likely to deal with in future research activities. In developing countries, some government offices, universities, and private firms may be equipped with main-frame computers of one type or another. However, the batch system dominates in these countries because of the scarcity of telephone facilities needed for interactive remote terminals. In addition, the availability of main-frame statistical software may be very limited because of high cost, and because of the scarcity of trained persons who can make the best use of them.

For these reasons, microcomputers may become more popular among researchers in both developed and developing countries. First, they are much cheaper than main-frame computers. Second, their software, in disk or cassette form, is much cheaper and easier to transport from one location to another, along with the microcomputer itself. Rapid progress is being made in the capability and availability of a wide range of software for microcomputers. The capability of a microcomputer and the software available with it may be sufficient for the research activities of most individuals. Although it is important to gain exposure to main-frame computers, we consider microcomputers to be the most feasible option for research in a developing country.

For those who may be going back to work with main-frame computers, Francis (1981) presents differences in the analysis results and formats of the most popular statistical packages available for use in main-frame computers. To become familiar with main-frame software for statistical analyses, students should take statistics courses or other appropriate courses in which such software is used as class materials. With a basic knowledge of statistics and some familiarity with available software, the student can relatively easily follow a user's manual to expand his familiarity with computers before returning home. A knowledge of statistics is also needed to make good use of microcomputer software, although instructions for such software tend to be relatively easy to follow, compared with instructions for main-frame computer software.

Since computer hardware and software are changing rapidly, it may be difficult for researchers to keep abreast of new developments in their home countries. One way to keep constantly informed is to become a member of a computer technology professional society. One such organization is the Association for Computing Machinery (ACM). ACM has nine major publications, thirty-two Special Interest Groups, and, most important, nearly 100 chapters around the world. For more information, write: ACM, 11 West 42nd Street, New York, NY 10036; (212) 869-7440; Telex: 421686.

Data processing and data analysis must be major concerns for those who wish to do research in their home countries. Thus, it may be useful for students to make arrangements, before leaving for home, to send their data for processing and analyses to their U.S. institutions.

5.4. Publication

Scientists write and publish for various reasons; direct financial reward is not one of them. Only in rare cases do the authors of journal articles receive payment for their publications. In some fields, authors sometimes are asked to pay part of the cost of publishing their articles (called a "page charge"). Other journals may charge a "submission fee" to authors for reviewing a manuscript submitted for consideration.

The single most important reason for writing and publishing is directly related to the basic reason for doing research: to generate new knowledge. No matter how important the research topic, how elegant the experimental design, or how significant the results might be, the research is of no use and contributes nothing to science until the results are published. Therefore, it is not an overstatement to say that the publication of research results is an essential part of research, and one might even say that the ultimate goal of research is publication.

The generation and publication of scientific and technical information is particularly important for developing countries, in view of the huge disparity between the developing countries and the developed countries in the production of scientific literature. For example, of the more than 20,000 issues of serials in the biological sciences surveyed by Biosciences Information Service database (BIOSIS) in 1981, less than 15 percent came from the developing countries.

The following sections discuss the essential elements in deciding where to publish and in preparing manuscripts. They also briefly describe the manuscript submission and review processes.

5.4.1. Where to publish

In deciding where to submit a manuscript for publication, it is important to remember that if the manuscript is not appropriate for a journal, it will not be published. And even if it is published, it will not reach the audience for which it is intended (peers working in the same general area). Either case defeats the goal of research. To select an appropriate journal, the researcher must evaluate the manuscript and match it with the scope, subject orientation, and audience of prospective journals. In addition, the researcher may want to consider the prestige, the circulation, and the publication frequency of the journals.

Through literature research, reading of professional journals, and contact and consultation with professors or colleagues, one can develop a

Research and Publication

good idea of where to submit a manuscript. For further ideas, we suggest the following references, most of which are published annually:

- *Ulrich's International Periodicals Directory.* New York: R. R. Bowker Co.
- *Irregular Serials and Annuals: An International Directory.* New York: R. R. Bowker Co.
- *The Standard Periodical Directory.* New York: Oxbridge Publications.
- *Directory of Publishing Opportunities in Journals and Periodicals.* Chicago: Marquis Academic Media.
- *Science Citation Index.* Philadelphia: ISI Press, Institute for Scientific Information.
- Lyle, S.P. 1979. 'Authors' guides to scholarly periodicals' *Scholarly Publishing,* April, pp. 255-261.
- *World List of Scientific Periodicals.* 1963-1965. 4th ed. London: Butterworths Scientific Publications.

Ulrich's International Periodicals Directory contains a listing of 90,000 periodicals throughout the world in 385 subject areas and 170 countries. *Irregular Serials and Annuals,* an international directory, lists 30,000 serials, annuals, conference proceedings, and other publications issued irregularly or less than twice a year. *The Standard Periodical Directory* contains nearly 70,000 names and addresses of magazines, journals, government publications, transactions, and proceedings of scientific societies published in North America.

Directory of Publishing Opportunities in Journals and Periodicals contains nearly 3,500 journals in diversified areas. Journal entries include information on editorial address and telephone number, editorial description, audience, subject fields, manuscript requirements, author information, and disposition of manuscript. A sample entry from this directory is given in appendix C.

Lyle's paper provides a list and brief description of twenty-five authors' guides to periodicals in eight broad subject areas. For example, *Authors' guide to journals in the health field,* by D. B. Ardell (published by Hayworth Press), includes a comprehensive description of about 450 journals in the health field published both in the United States and abroad. Each entry includes information on manuscript location, index and abstract, types of articles published, preferred topic areas, manuscript review lag time, publication lag time for accepted manuscripts, acceptance rate, page charges, and manuscript style requirements. A sample entry from this guide is given in appendix D.

These references can be used to help the researcher match his manuscript to an appropriate journal and, to some extent, they are helpful as guides to preparing the manuscript to meet the individual journal's requirements. *Science Citation Index* publishes *Annual Citation Reports,* which can assist in assessing the comparative prestige of scientific journals. Under the Corporate Index section of *The Science Citation Index,* it is possible to determine what journals are available in any given country.

Whether to publish a paper in one's home country, or in one's own language, or whether to publish internationally is difficult to decide. To gain international visibility and reach a larger audience, it is important to do the latter; however, to achieve scientific and technological independence gradually, it is important to do the former. In any case, we suggest that if the research deals with uniquely local problems, then the researcher should consider publishing it in his own language and country. Although most journals do not accept manuscripts that have been published elsewhere, it is possible to publish such manuscripts, with some modifications, also in a second language, for example, in English. This is particularly important if the contribution is of worldwide significance. If the work is likely to lead to further research of wider implication, it should then be presented and published in a different forum.

A cover letter should be sent with the manuscript. Most journals acknowledge the receipt of a manuscript. If no acknowledgment is received in a reasonable period of time, such as two to four weeks, one should write the editorial office to make sure that the manuscript was not lost in the mail.

5.4.2. The review process

The general policies, procedures, and criteria involved in the manuscript review process are similar for most respectable journals, and familiarity with policies and procedures should enhance the manuscript preparation and the rate of acceptance. After receiving a manuscript, the editor will decide whether the subject is suitable for the journal. He then checks to be certain that the manuscript conforms to the journal's requirements and style. The next step is to send the manuscript to one or more reviewers (or referees). The reviewers are usually scientists and experts in the appropriate field. Based on the reviewers' recommendations, the editor will accept, reject, or return the manuscript for modification. Obviously, reviewers are a very important group of scientists since they help to assure not only the quality of publication, but also the quality and advancement of science.

The author of a manuscript that is accepted for publication should be proud because (1) the research is essentially completed (although it may be another two to twelve months before the manuscript is in print), (2) a contribution has been made to the field of science, and (3) only a small percentage (perhaps 5 percent to 20 percent among prestigious journals) of unsolicited manuscripts are accepted.

Frequently, the manuscript will be returned with reviewers' comments and suggestions for modification of the manuscript. Generally, the writer should accept the reviewers' comments and suggestions. Revising the manuscript should be considered a learning experience, and comments should be studied carefully. The chances are that these comments will help to improve the quality of the manuscript, and they may sometimes provide new perspectives on data interpretation or research direction. As much as possible, all the suggested changes should be incorporated; then the revised manuscript should be resubmitted with a cover sheet providing a point-by-point response to or disposition of all reviewers' comments.

Most of the respectable journals have rejection rates exceeding 50 percent. Thus, the writer should not be surprised if the editor sends a letter of regret, saying that the manuscript is "unacceptable." This is especially true if the author is an inexperienced researcher-author. The author may be angry, disappointed, or depressed, but should not be discouraged. The reviewers' comments should be examined carefully, critically, and objectively. Rewriting may require additional experiments and reanalysis and interpretation of the data, but this should be done. Then, the much improved manuscript can be resubmitted, preferably to a different journal. If the work is truly significant and can be defended scientifically, it will eventually become a published paper.

Most journals have instructions or guidelines for reviewers. If the author understands these guidelines this increases the chances that his manuscript will be accepted. The following are the kinds of questions that reviewers are asked to keep in mind as they review manuscripts:

- Is the particular research question or subject important?
- Does the paper contribute to new knowledge?
- Is the work original or timely?
- Is the approach, method, or experimental design appropriate?
- Are the conclusions properly supported?
- Is the analysis of data or interpretation of results sound?
- Does the abstract convey the paper's meaning?
- Is the paper well organized?
- Does the paper cover the subject adequately and concisely?
- Is the language simple and effective?
- Does the paper adhere to style set forth in "Instructions to authors"?
- Are the tables and figures clear and useful?

- Are the references complete?
- Is the subject appropriate for the journal?
- Is statistical treatment of the data appropriate?

Usually there is separate space on the manuscript review form for the reviewers' general recommendations as to acceptance, modification, or rejection. On a separate sheet or form, the reviewer is asked to cite specific deficiencies in the manuscript and to provide suggestions for improvement; these will be sent to the author without identifying the reviewer's name.

5.4.3. Manuscript preparation

The manuscript should be prepared in the standard style specified by the journal. Style instructions are often available from the editor, or they can be found somewhere in the journal. The latest issue of the journal can be studied for style requirements, or the author can refer to the *Directory of Publishing Opportunities in Journals and Periodicals* for an individual journal's style requirements.

There are three major style manuals for science writing in English that are used by many U.S. journals, directly or indirectly; these are the manuals prepared by the American Psychological Association (1974), University of Chicago Press (1983), and Modern Language Association (1970). *How to write and publish a scientific paper,* by R. A. Day (1979), although written as a guide for scientific writing in English, is useful for scientific writing in any language. Besides detailed "how to" information from title to illustration, Day's book also deals with such basic matters as manuscript type, submission, and publishing. We recommend this book to everyone.

Although different journals may have different specific requirements in style, especially with respect to figure and table preparation and reference style, the essential elements and objectives for a readable, logical, clear, and concise scientific documentation are the same. The commonly accepted organizational elements for a scientific paper are given below. (For details, refer to the "Guide for authors" in specific journals or to the major style manuals just mentioned.)

Title. Titles should be brief, specific, informative, and appropriate for indexing and retrieval purposes. Some journals limit the length of the title to fifty (English) characters, including the spaces between words.

Authors' names. The author's full names and their addresses should be listed; the address is normally the location where the research was conducted. If the current address is different, it should be included in a footnote.

Abstract. The abstract should be concise and to the point. It should describe the scope and purpose, methods or procedures, significant new results, and conclusions. This should be done in no more than 250 (English) words, sometimes much less (e.g., *Science* requires an abstract of 50 to 75 words). The abstract should be written for literature searchers as well as for journal readers. Some journals also require that the author supply a list of key words or descriptors for indexing and information retrieval purposes. It is worth remembering that the abstract is sometimes called a brief, a summary, or a synopsis.

Introduction. The introduction should briefly describe (1) the subject and its relationship to previous work and references, (2) the scope and purpose, (3) the plan of presentation, and (4) the value to the reader.

Materials and methods or methods of investigation. The methods, the equipment, and the materials used should be described in sufficient detail to permit the work to be repeated by other investigators. Only new techniques need to be described in detail, but known or standard methods should be referred to adequately. Deviations from standards should be noted, if there are any.

Results. Data should be presented concisely and clearly, using tables and illustrations if necessary. Adequate indication of the level of experimental error and the statistical significance of results should be given. The same information should not be presented in both tables and figures (graphs or line drawings). Complete documentation need not be presented if the data are voluminous, but complete documentation should be available in cited references.

Discussion. The discussion considers the meaning of the data or the interpretation of results. The discussion should include (1) the principles and relationships, (2) generalizations within the scope of the study, (3) comparisons of results and interpretations with previously published work (with references), (4) the theoretical and practical implications, and (5) the significance of the study-research.

Conclusions. The conclusions should end the paper, and they should review or state concisely the significant implications of the data presented in the body of the paper. (In some cases, it may be more appropriate to substitute the heading "summary and conclusions" for the heading "conclusions.")

Acknowledgments. An acknowledgments section may be included to give recognition for significant help or financial assitance received in the course of the work. Some funding agencies require the acknowledgment of their financial support. Some journals specify that financial support be acknowledged at the end of the References section.

Literature cited or references. The purpose of this section is to acknowledge the various sources from which ideas and information were borrowed. For the benefit of the reader, (1) only relevant and significant references should be listed, (2) all references cited in the text should be listed, and (3) all references should be identified in such a way that they can be located easily by the reader.

There are many ways of handling references, and journals vary considerably in their reference style requirements. The three most common styles are—

- Name and year system: The references are listed alphabetically in the reference section and cited by name and year of publication, for example, "Lee 1970."
- Citation order system: The references are cited in the order they appear in the paper and numbered in the reference section accordingly.
- Alphabet-number system: The references are cited by numbers from a numbered, alphabetized (by authors' names) list of references.

If uncertain of which reference style to use, the author should ask for a "Guide for authors" or study the latest issue of the journal to which the paper will be submitted. Private communications may not be listed as references in some journals. In general, the use of "anonymous" in the reference section should be avoided.

The general organization and style governing scientific writing will apply in report preparation, except that the author can list more exhaustive references and complete documentation of the data is required. Because some funding agencies may have specific requirements, their instructions (as to title page, grant or project number, etc.) should be carefully followed. An executive summary and a section on recommended future research may also be included, when appropriate.

5.5. Epilogue

Many aspects of this chapter may be far from the reality each individual will face on returning home. We did not write this chapter with only the contribution of young researchers in mind. We believe that those who read these chapters will be the leaders in their countries' development in the sciences for many years to come. Those who are in the United States as students should absorb as much knowledge as they can, not only for the

Research and Publication

immediate needs of their countries, but also for their long-run future needs. The principles of science are timeless and universal among all of us who are engaging in scientific research. Variation exists in the technological facilities and the materials available, depending on the country and the office or laboratory to which the student is returning.

Each reader knows better than anyone else the conditions of the workplace he will return to upon completion of his stay in the United States. Knowing those conditions, he should make appropriate modifications in some of the points we suggested here. Knowing what is not available in the home country and knowing what is available in the United States, the student can make some future plans while still in the United States. For instance, he might explore the possibility of research collaboration between his home organizations and U.S. scientists. He might explore the possibility of having U.S. scholars he has met assist in developing research facilities in the home institution or organization, or he might explore the possibility of obtaining services such as library computer literature searches and data processing or analysis from his U.S. institution.

Scientific research has been conducted for many years without computers and other modern tools. If a place of work does not have computer facilities, this does not mean that researchers there will not be able to conduct good research. Without computer facilities or without sophisticated laboratory facilities, conducting high quality research may be a real challenge, and the great differences between facilities available in the home country and in the United States may be discouraging. Nevertheless, it is the returned professionals and scientists who hold the key to the future direction of research activities. Research may have to be conducted within the facilities available in home institutions, or it might be done with some assistance from the contacts established while in the United States. It will be possible to make suggestions as to what facilities home institutions should obtain in the near future and what training should be given to future scholars to strengthen the research capability of the home country. But, all of this is possible only if future researchers learn as much as they can about research and publication while still in the United States.

Upon returning home, each individual will need to make a great effort not to become isolated as a researcher. Communication with the world's community of scientists must be kept open through access to others' publications, by attending international professional meetings, and, if possible, by collaboration with scientists of other countries, particularly those in the United States. Another chapter in this book, *"The scientist or scholar interacts: Communication and interpersonal relations in the developing countries,"* provides suggestions on establishing and maintaining communication with other scientists before and after returning to the home country.

Acknowledgment

The authors acknowledge the assistance of the following persons for their valuable comments and suggestions: Dr. Altay Birand, professor of civil engineering, Middle East Technical University, Ankara, Turkey; Mr. Cheick Drame, head of sociology division, Office Malien de Betail et de Viande (National Office for Cattle and Meat), Mali; Mr. Mohamed El-Ezaby, assistant lecturer, Department of Rural Sociology, University of Alexandria, Egypt.

The authors are grateful for the information provided by Professor Dale Grosvenor, Iowa State University Computation Center and Computer Science Department, based on his experiences in Nigeria, Indonesia, and Zambia.

References Cited

American Psychological Association. 1974. *Publication manual of the American Psychological Association,* Washington, D.C.: American Psychological Association.

Babbie, Earl. 1983. *The practice of social research,* Belmont, Calif.: Wadsworth Publishing Company.

Bailey, Kenneth D. 1978. *Methods of social research,* 2d ed. New York: Academic Press.

Blalock, Ann Bonar, and Hubert M. Blalock, Jr. 1982. *Introduction to social research,* 2d ed. Englewood Cliffs, N. J.: Prentice-Hall.

Campbell, Donald, and Julian Stanley. 1963. *Experimental and quasi-experimental designs for research.* Chicago: Rand McNally.

Day, R. A. 1979. *How to write and publish a scientific paper.* Philadelphia: ISI Press.

Francis, Ivor. 1981. *Statistical software: A comparative review.* New York: North Holland.

Holsti, Ole. 1969. *Content analysis for the social sciences and humanities.* Reading, Mass.: Addison-Wesley.

Isaac, Stephen, and William B. Michael. 1981. *Handbook in research and evaluation,* 2d ed. San Diego, Calif.: Edits Publishers.

Kish, Leslie. 1965. *Survey sampling.* New York: John Wiley.

Medawar, P. B. 1979. *Advice to a young scientist.* New York: Harper & Row Publishers.

Modern Language Association. 1970. *MLA style sheet.* New York: Modern Language Association.

Ott, Lyman. 1977. *An introduction to statistical methods and data analysis.* North Scituate, Mass.: Duxbury Press.

Ott, Lyman, William Mendenhall, and Richard F. Lawson. 1978. *Statistics: A tool for the social sciences.* North Scituate, Mass.: Duxbury Press.

Research and Publication

Rossi, Peter H., and Howard E. Freeman. 1982. *Evaluation: A systematic approach,* 2d ed. Beverly Hills, Calif.: Sage Publications.

Shaffir, William, Robert Stebbins, and Allan Turowetz. 1980. *Field work experience: Qualitative approaches to social research.* New York: St. Martin's Press.

Smith, Robert V. 1980. *Development and management of research groups: A guide for university researchers.* Austin, Tex.: University of Texas Press.

Spradley, James. 1980. *Participant observation.* New York: Holt, Rinehart, and Winston.

Spradley, James. 1979. *The ethnographic interview.* New York: Holt, Rinehart, and Winston.

Stinchcombe, Arthur. 1978. *Theoretical methods in social history.* New York: Academic Press.

United Nations. 1973. *Research proposals: A guide for scientists, technologists and research institutes in developing countries.* New York: United Nations.

University of Chicago. 1972. *A manual of style.* Chicago: University of Chicago.

White, V. P. 1975. *Grants: How to find out about them and what to do next.* New York: Plenum Press.

Research and Publication

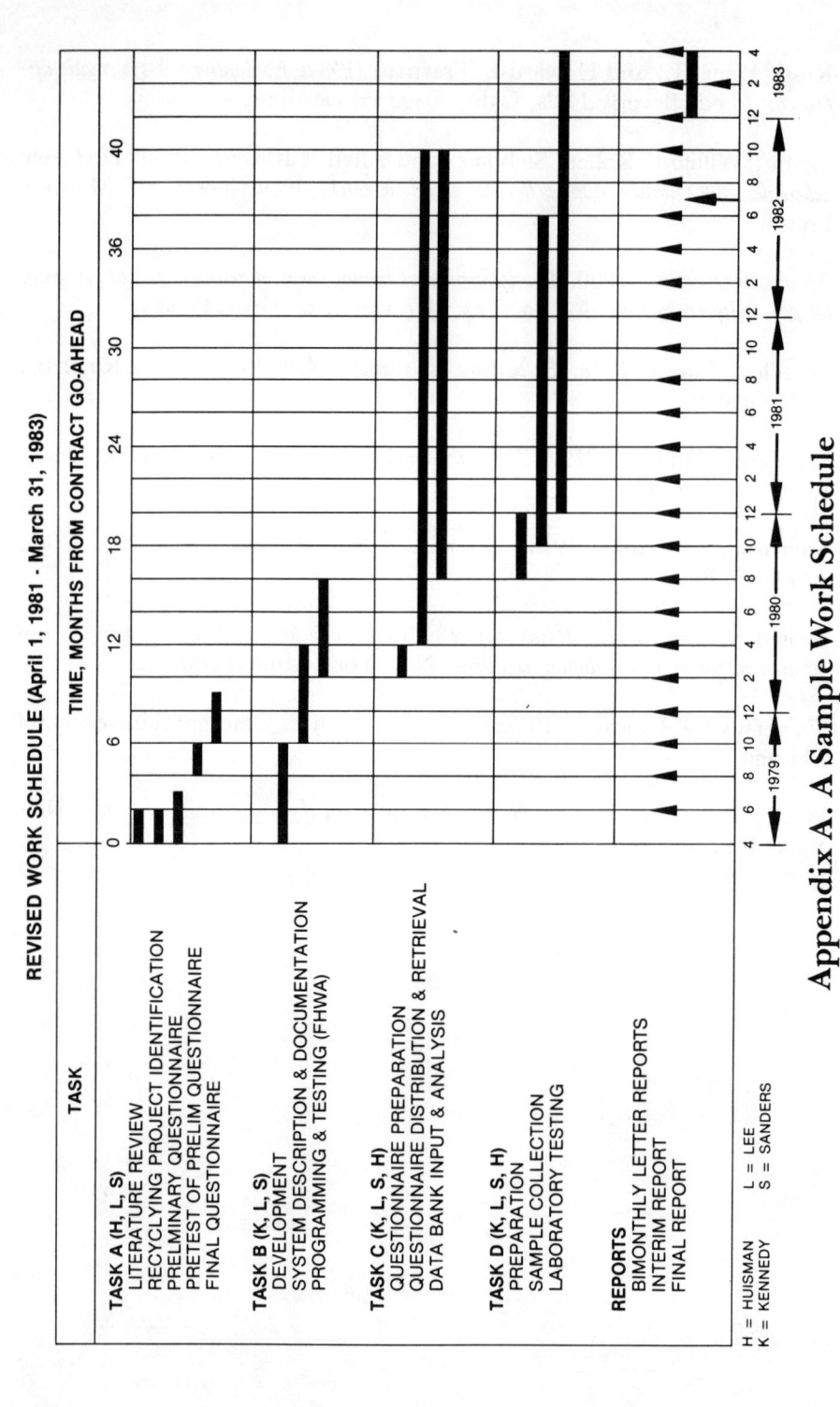

REVISED WORK SCHEDULE (April 1, 1981 - March 31, 1983)

TASK	TIME, MONTHS FROM CONTRACT GO-AHEAD
TASK A (H, L, S) LITERATURE REVIEW RECYCLYING PROJECT IDENTIFICATION PRELMINARY QUESTIONNAIRE PRETEST OF PRELIM QUESTIONNAIRE FINAL QUESTIONNAIRE	
TASK B (K, L, S) DEVELOPMENT SYSTEM DESCRIPTION & DOCUMENTATION PROGRAMMING & TESTING (FHWA)	
TASK C (K, L, S, H) QUESTIONNAIRE PREPARATION QUESTIONNAIRE DISTRIBUTION & RETRIEVAL DATA BANK INPUT & ANALYSIS	
TASK D (K, L, S, H) PREPARATION SAMPLE COLLECTION LABORATORY TESTING	
REPORTS BIMONTHLY LETTER REPORTS INTERIM REPORT FINAL REPORT	

H = HUISMAN   L = LEE
K = KENNEDY   S = SANDERS

Appendix A. A Sample Work Schedule

Research and Publication

Appendix B. A sample page from *Grants Register* (1981-1983)

Further information from:
   Imperial Optical Company Ltd.
   Hermant Building, 21 Dundas Square
   Toronto, Ontario M5B 1B7
   Canada

[918]
INDEPENDENT BROADCASTING AUTHORITY, (U.K.)
IBA Fellowships/Grants

Purpose: To further the study of the relationship between education and television or local radio.

No. offered: Three or four Fellowships at any one time.

Value: Recipient's salary and superannuation, and in some cases a living allowance, are paid for the period of secondment, plus reimbursement for additional approved expenses.

Tenable at appropriate institutions in the United Kingdom.

Eligibility: Open to experienced and qualified individuals working in the United Kingdom.

Note: The award is subject to release on secondment being agreed upon by the candidate's employer.
   Whereas Fellowships are chiefly allocated in relation to the educational use of broadcasting, Fellowships and Grants are also given periodically in other aspects of broadcasting.

Further information from:
   Education Department
   Independent Broadcasting Authority
   70 Brompton Road
   London SW3 IEY
   England.

[919]
INDIAN COUNCIL FOR CULTURAL RELATIONS
INDIAN GOVERNMENT
Jawaharial Nehru Award for International Understanding

An annual Award of 100,000 rupees and a citation is given in recognition of outstanding contribution toward the promotion of international understanding, goodwill and friendship among peoples of the world. Awardees may be persons of any nationality, race, creed or sex. Candidates may be nominated for work achieved within five years immediately preceding the nomination, or for earlier work, the significance of which has only recently become apparent. Proposals may be submitted by leaders of international organizations and institutions, academicians, heads of Indian missions abroad, heads of learned societies and research institutions, or any other persons whom the jury feels to be competent to make nominations.

Closing date: 31st August of the year for which the Award is to be given.

Further information from:
   Jawarharial Nehru Award for
      International Understanding
   Secretary, Indian Council for Cultural
      Relations
   Azad Bhavan
   Indraprastha Estate
   New Delhi
   India.

[920]
INDIAN COUNCIL OF MEDICAL RESEARCH
Medical Research Prizes

The Council offers numerous awards, ranging in value from 500 rupees to 5,000 rupees each. Prizes are in the broad field of medical research and cover the following areas: internal medicine, community medicine, leprosy, eye diseases, cancer, nutrition, cardiovascular disease, microbiology, bio-medical science, and dermatology. Eligibility is open to Indian residents engaged in medical research in India. Nominations may be submitted by principals and officers of Indian medical colleges, research institutes, and universities.

Further information from:
   Indian Council of Medical Research
   P.O. Box 4508
   Ansari Nagar
   New Delhi 110016
   India.

[921]
INDIAN COUNCIL OF SOCIAL SCIENCE RESEARCH
Research Fellowships and Grants

The following annual awards are available for research to be carried out at approved institutions, usually in India. The awards

Appendix C. A sample entry from *Directory of Publishing Opportunities in Journals and Periodicals*

CHEMICAL ENGINEERING JOURNAL [2467]
An International Journal of Research and Development
Elsevier Sequoia SA
P.O. Box 851
CH-1001 Lausanne 1, Switzerland
(021) 20 73 81

SUBSCRIPTION DATA
First published in 1970.

Issues and rates: Published bi-monthly. Articles per average issue: 9. Annual rate(s): Sfr. 330.00.

EDITORIAL DESCRIPTION
Contains papers of relevance to chemical engineering (original research work not previously published, reviews on recent developments). Criteria for acceptance of papers are originality of thought, quality of work and clarity of style.

MANUSCRIPT INFORMATION

Subject field(s): Chemical engineering.

Manuscript requirements: See latest issue for style requirements. Submit 3 copies, with abstract.

Author information and reprints: Payment in reprints only. Simultaneous submission is not permitted. Periodical holds exclusive rights after acceptance. Copyright held by publication. Reprints available at cost.

Disposition of manuscript: Receipt acknowledged. Decision in 8-12 weeks. Published 4-5 months after acceptance. Rejections returned.

Submit to: The Publisher or B. A. Buffham: D.C. Freshwater, Editors Loughborough University of Technology Loughborough, Leies., LE11 3TV, U.K. (5093) 63171

SPECIAL STIPULATIONS
Papers should be submitted to an appropriate associate editor chosen on the basis of subject matter, language and geography. See inside cover of the journal.

Research and Publication

Appendix D.   A sample entry from *Authors' Guide to Journals in the Health Field*

JOURNAL TITLE:	**NEW SOCIETY**
MANUSCRIPT ADDRESS:	30 Southampton Street London WC2E 7HE England
SUBSCRIPTION ADDRESS:	Paul Barker New Science Publications 128 Longacre - London WC2 England
ANNUAL SUBSCRIPTION RATE:	$44 Individual; $44 Institutional
INDEXED/ABSTRACTED IN:	Not Given
CIRCULATION/FREQUENCY:	30,000/Weekly
TYPES OF ARTICLES:	Research, case studies
PREFERRED CONTENT AREAS:	Adolescent health care; child health services; community health services; consumerism & health care; day care; environmental health; family health services; geriatric care; health care delivery systems; health surveys; laws/legislation & health care; malpractice; Medicare/Medicaid; patient relations; planning; health; preventive health; psychosocial patient care/services; public welfare & health services; social medicine; social services & patient care; voluntary health organizations.

MANUSCRIPT COPIES:	1	PAGE CHARGES:	No
REVIEW PERIOD:	1 month	STYLE REQUIREMENTS:	Chicago
PUBLICATION TIME:	1-12 months	STYLE SHEET:	No
EARLY PUBLICATION OPTION:	No	REVISED THESES:	Acceptable
ACCEPTANCE RATE:	5%	STUDENT PAPERS:	No
AUTHORSHIP RESTRICTIONS:	None	REPRINT POLICY:	None

Research and Publication

Appendix E.   A sample authors' guide, *Journals of the American Society of Civil Engineers*

TECHNICAL PAPERS

Original papers should be submitted in triplicate to the Manager of Technical and Professional Publications, ASCE, 345 East 47th Street, New York, N.Y. 10017. Authors must indicate the Technical Division or Council, Technical Committee, Subcommittee, and Task Committee (if any) to which the paper should be referred. Those who are planning to submit material will expedite the review and publication procedures by complying with the following basic requirements:

1. Titles must have a length not exceeding 50 characters and spaces.

2. The manuscript (an original ribbon copy and two duplicate copies) should be double-spaced on one side of 8-1/2-in. (220-mm) by 11-in. (280-mm) paper. Three copies of all figures and tables must be included.

3. Generally, the maximum length of a paper is 10,000 word-equivalents. As an *approximation,* each full manuscript page of text, tables or figures is the equivalent of 300 words. If a particular subject cannot be adequately presented within the 10,000-word limit, the paper should be accompanied by a rationale for the overlength. This will permit rapid review and approval by the Division or Council Publications and Executive Committees and the Society's Committee on Publications. Valuable contributions to the Society's publications are not intended to be discouraged by this procedure.

4. The author's full name, Society membership grade, and a footnote stating present employment must appear on the first page of the paper. Authors need not be Society members.

5. All mathematics must be typewritten and special symbols must be identified properly. The letter symbols used should be defined where they first appear, in figures, tables, or text, and arranged alphabetically in an appendix at the end of the paper titled Appendix.—Notation.

6. Standard definitions and symbols should be used. Reference should be made to the lists published by the American National Standards Institute and to the *Authors' Guide to the Publications of ASCE.*

7. Figures should be drawn in black ink, at a size that, with a 50% reduction, would have a published width in the *Journals* of from 3 in. (76 mm) to 4-1/2 in. (110 mm). The lettering must be legible at the reduced size. Photographs should be submitted as glossy prints. Explanations and descriptions must be placed in text rather than within the figure.

8. Tables should be typed (an original ribbon copy and two duplicates) on one side of 8-1/2-in. (220-mm) by 11-in. (280-mm) paper. An explanation of each table must appear in the text.

9. References cited in text should be arranged in alphabetical order in an appendix at the end of the paper, or preceding the Appendix.—Notation, as an Appendix.—References.

10. A list of key words and an information retrieval abstract of 175 words should be provided with each paper.

11. A summary of approximately 40 words must accompany the paper.

12. A set of conclusions must end the paper.

13. Dual units, i.e., U.S. Customary followed by SI (International System) units in parentheses, should be used throughout the paper.

14. A practical applications section should be included also, if appropriate.

6.

Developing a Resource Library

Harold Borko
Eileen Goldstein

6.1. Introduction

Libraries and information resources can plan an important role in helping integrate students from the developing world into both the academic environment of developed countries when studying abroad and professional positions in the home country upon return. The basic resources in a library collection include books, journals, pamphlets, directories, standards, patents, and conference proceedings, but bibliographic material alone will not meet the information needs of all users. Saracevic, Braga, and Solis (1979) classify the information needed in developing countries as follows:

1. know-how information
2. know-why information
3. show-how information

While both know-how and know-why information are generally found in basic library resources, some of this material will need to be repackaged to conform to local conditions and customs. Show-how information, however, is operational and is generally oriented to specific training needs in a localized area; it is usually not found in the published literature. Slamecka and McCarn (1979) also make a distinction between recorded information and personal contact; they refer to the latter as "experiential in-

Developing a Resource Library

formation," which is generally obtained through experts. Thus, resource libraries in developing countries need more than bibliographic materials to supply sufficient appropriate information.

A resource library in a developing country serves several functions:

1. It collects and serves as a repository of literature about the native country. This collection covers such topics as politics, economics, science, agriculture, and technology and should naturally include materials produced in the native language as well as foreign language documents written about the country.
2. It collects and disseminates up-to-date information on various academic disciplines and areas of specialization for use by students, professors, researchers, and professionals.
3. It helps prospective students select appropriate schools for study abroad and provides information about courses of study, entrance and graduation requirements, scholarships, housing, and the general social and cultural environment of countries abroad.
4. It provides students with information about the cities and countries in which they wish to study and helps them avoid culture shock.
5. It assists in adapting knowledge-information acquired abroad to local needs and conditions.
6. It helps returning students reintegrate into their society and mitigates reverse culture shock of students who may have become accustomed to a more developed informational infrastructure while studying abroad.

6.2. Library Information Resources

Various categories of library-information materials are needed for the resource library to achieve the objectives listed above. These include published and ephemeral* material about the country and local community; a basic collection of reference materials in science, technology, social science, arts, and humanities; catalogs of and information on both domestic and foreign universities; and various other bibliographic and non-bibliographic tools useful for workers in the community.

6.2.1. Repository of local information

It is essential that at least one resource library in every country, developed or developing, be a repository library and collect all published

---

*Ephemeral materials have short-lived value, are generally in limited circulation, and are not copyrighted.

and, if possible, all relevant ephemeral materials pertaining to that country and to the local area in which the library is located. The repository library should receive all published material from government offices and documents from foreign countries; the latter can usually be acquired by an exchange agreement. If there are national laws relating to copyright procedures, commercial publishers who wish to copyright their publications can generally be required to give one or two copies of these documents to a repository library. However, both Shepard (1963) and Krzys and Litton (1975) mention problems related to legal deposit for copyright purposes; regulations are confusing, the state often does not implement the requirements, and definitions are lacking as to the type of material included. Finally, a resource library needs to maintain a comprehensive collection of documents about its own country for reference purposes. This is not an easy task; poor bibliographic control and lack of union catalogs* make it difficult for librarians and information specialists in developing countries to collect materials published in their own countries. In fact, Saracevic (1980) notes that librarians in developing countries often have better control over the materials published abroad, because of the availability of various indexes and catalogs than they have over locally produced material.

Citizens going abroad, and especially students who will be studying abroad, are unofficial ambassadors of their countries. They will be asked many questions about life in their countries. They should be well informed, and therefore they need access to current information about local conditions before going abroad. A repository library can serve a central role in providing that needed information.

6.2.2. Collection development

A primary function of a resource library in a developing country is to meet the basic information needs of its users in specific scientific and technical areas. While it is beyond the scope of this chapter to discuss procedures for library acquisition and collection development, a few basic suggestions can be made. A number of books have been written on these topics, and several citations listed at the end of the chapter in the bibliography on collection development may prove useful. In general, a resource library should try to acquire an appropriate and varied selection of information materials. The following list identifies the types of materials that might be useful in collection development:

1. a basic reference collection, including dictionaries, directories, handbooks;

---

*A union catalog is a listing that combines, in alphabetical order, the holdings of more than one library.

2. a core collection of books;
3. a core collection of selected technical reports;
4. a core collection of journals;
5. a core collection of conference proceedings;
6. selected abstracting and indexing services;
7. relevant dissertations and theses, particularly those by returned graduates;
8. patents;
9. translations;
10. information about research in progress and meetings; and
11. catalogs of publications.

The extent of the collections and the inclusion of different types of materials will vary with the needs of each library or information center and the allotted budget. A selection and acquisition policy will help set priorities in areas of interest; various books and guides are available to aid in developing policies, and several are included in the collection development bibliography at the conclusion of this chapter.

6.2.3. University catalogs and related information

A resource library in a developing country should maintain up-to-date files of information on selected institutions of higher learning appropriate to the needs of both the native country and the prospective students. The files should provide information on—

- study programs in the sciences, humanities, and professions located in selected universities, domestic and foreign;

- entry prerequisites for study abroad, such as minimum competencies in English or other languages, as well as all additional requirements;

- details on school and living expenses, including sources of financial aid, scholarships, and housing. This type of information can generally be obtained by writing directly to the institutions and asking them to include the resource library in all future mailings, by contacting the information sections of foreign country embassies, or by contacting local citizens who may have received training at a specific institution.

6.2.4. Information to minimize culture shock

Culture shock is normally experienced by almost everyone making an extended visit to a foreign country. It can be a pleasant experience characterized by excitement in learning about new places, people, and customs. It can also be an unpleasant experience if the visitor does not know what to expect and is frightened by the strangeness of the situation. The resource library can help minimize the undesirable effects of culture shock by providing the student going abroad with—

- information about local cultures abroad (e.g., food, dress, housing, entertainment, social activities),
- specific information about the areas in which schools of interest are located (e.g., student population, community resources, points of interest),
- a list of names and local addresses of returned graduates from various institutions abroad.

6.2.5. Information on needs of the home country

The resource library can help the student going abroad keep in touch with the home community by disseminating to the student information relating to local developments and activities in the student's area of specialization. By keeping informed about local needs and conditions, the student should be better able to adapt his academic studies to the requirements of the sponsoring country and local community. This information on home country developments and activities should also provide valuable insight for the student in collecting bibliographic materials and identifying valuable extracurricular activities, such as conferences and lectures. Such information can also lessen the likelihood of extreme reentry problems upon return to the home country.

6.2.6. Information for mitigating reverse culture shock

Students often face problems upon returning to their home countries when they begin to work, or try to continue their studies, without the advanced facilities found in developed countries. The major universities in countries where the students have studied usually have large and varied bibliographic collections and access to an even greater variety of materials through established interlibrary loan programs. In addition, these university libraries provide access to computerized databases, both bibliographic and numeric, and to technical reports from government, educational, and research institutions. Such resources are often lacking in developing countries or, at least, they are not as plentiful or technologically advanced. This can be a very frustrating situation for the young professional who has just completed his academic studies in a richly endowed environment and suddenly finds himself unable to use newly acquired skills in his home country, where conditions differ. Developing countries cannot build facilities equal to those found in the United States or other developed countries in the near future because of a lack of money, staff, materials, and adequate housing. However, resource libraries in the developing world can help lessen the return culture shock by maintaining adequate core collections with reference tools and key works, as well as information on where other material is available and the know-how to get information quickly. The success of the resource library often depends, however, on the support of individuals such as the student trained in a developed country.

6.3. The Student's Role in Collection Development

The relationship between users and the resource library should be mutually supportive. That is, while the resource library supplies needed information for users, the users should assume active roles in the maintenance and development of the library's collection. The active participation of users, both as students and later as professionals, will help improve the quality of the resource library and the services it is able to provide.

There are several reasons for encouraging students and professionals who have studied abroad to assist in the development and maintenance of resource libraries in their home countries. First, user participation in collection development and maintenance helps ensure that the available resources will actually meet the users' needs. Also, the users' specialized knowledge and access to numerous resources in the developed countries make user contributions to library resource development especially valuable.

A second reason for encouraging students and professionals to assist in collection development is the generally acknowledged shortage of library and information specialists who can perform the task of collection development in developing countries. For example, the *Encyclopedia of library and information services* estimates that Mexico needs approximately 7,000 library-information specialists, according to U.S. standards (Krzys and Litton 1975). Furthermore, the available library-information specialists spend much of their time on the classification and cataloging of bibliographic materials (Asheim 1966; McCarthy 1975; Lemos 1981). Since bibliographic materials are lacking in many developing countries (Keren and Harmon 1980; Krevitt Eres 1981), one might conclude that collection development is not sufficiently emphasized by library-information specialists in such countries.

A third reason why nationals studying abroad should help acquire library materials is that such aid would expedite the acquisitions process. Having adequate library resources is especially important for professionals or researchers requiring up-to-date information quickly. If the material is not available locally, or at least easily and properly identifiable, users may have to wait several months to obtain the desired information. The long delay in acquiring bibliographic materials from other countries is attributed to several factors including tight budgetary constraints, administrative controls, problems with mail and transportation, changes in exchange rates, and the difficulty in obtaining hard currency. Students living abroad could help alleviate some of these problems if they were encouraged to act as agents of the resource library in collection development.

Students may assist in maintaining and developing the collections of their resource libraries through various activities prior to departure, during their stay, before returning to their native countries, and upon their return.

6.3.1. Prior to departure

The student should familiarize himself with available resources in his field of specialization prior to leaving the home country. First he needs to become aware of existing published materials in his area of specialization that are available in libraries in the native country. To accomplish this, the student might review lists and guides, such as Herner's *Brief guide to sources of scientific and technical information* (1980), and then check to see if any of this material is presently in the resource library collection. The student might also consult his national council of science and technology (or a similar agency) to see if lists of core collections have been compiled in his country.

To review existing collections in his country, the student will probably have to visit several libraries since union catalogs, even if they exist, are usually not current. When a specific organization is responsible for funding, the student should go first to the library of that organization. When the government is the sponsor or when personal funds will be used to finance study abroad, the student should visit either the national council of science and technology, a nearby university library, or the national library. The resource library should have a general list of other libraries in the country identifying where collections in various disciplines or specializations exist. It is as important to identify what does not exist as it is to identify what does exist.

Another task for the student to perform prior to departure is to make contact with a library-information specialist in the funding organization, in the national library, or in the hometown library. The student should remain in contact with this specialist during his stay abroad regarding the selection and possible purchase of material.

6.3.2. During the stay abroad

The selection of material by visiting students is particularly difficult because of the large quantity of information available, and because of problems with both searching for and reading documents in foreign languages. Wellisch (1973) notes that a person is greatly hindered when searching both manual and computerized indexes and abstracts in a second language. Use and selection of information resources is made more difficult by the fact that students from developing countries generally have not had the same background in the use of libraries as have students from more developed countries, and they are often unfamiliar with the seemingly complicated retrieval systems. Visiting students might consider taking some of the courses designed to facilitate library use and information retrieval that are offered at many universities. Saracevic (1980) recommends providing foreign students with supplemental education in the availability and utilization of scientific and technical information, as well as in the use of information tools and systems.

While there has been little emphasis on training students in the use of libraries, UNESCO has funded special programs on library use and information retrieval procedures for scientists and engineers from the developing world. One such program was the International Conference on Education and Training of Engineers and Higher Technicians, held in New Delhi in 1976. Both Adams (1975) and Saracevic (1980) mention efforts to teach practicing professionals in developing countries to become more efficient in the use of information resources.

Despite the difficulties already mentioned, students should continually identify, select, and acquire relevant information resource materials throughout their studies abroad. Aside from searching on their own, students may acquire valuable informational materials from classes or extracurricular professional activities. Ideally, students' scholarships or budgets should cover the purchase of all relevant course materials, such as textbooks and syllabi. It would also be useful for students to joint appropriate professional organizations, which usually send bulletins or journals to members at reduced rates.

Other important sources for identifying relevant bibliographic materials are lists obtained through coursework, such as the reading lists supplied by many professors and the bibliographies prepared by students for class assignments. Both could be helpful as guides for identifying and selecting materials for use in resource libraries at home. Reading lists and bibliographies obtained during the student's stay may be sent directly to the library-information specialist with whom the student should be maintaining contact. Students should also send brochures and catalogs from the school to the resource librarian to help keep the university file current at the resource library.

Students might also consider contacting their embassies or, more specifically, the education or scientific attachés working at the embassies for guidance and support in collecting relevant bibliographic material. Brazil, for example, has developed a procedure for obtaining documents through scientific attachés working in developed countries (Adams 1975). Communication between the home country and the education or scientific attaché is usually well established through telex, phone calls, visits, and mail pouches. If arrangements have been made previously with the education or scientific attachés, students might work together with them in acquiring bibliographic materials and sending them home.

As mentioned previously, bibliographic material alone will not meet all of the information needs of professionals in the developing world. Since personal contact is apparently very important, the student should actively try to identify key people in his field, working in or near the university, and make contact with them. These key people may later be able to help the young professional by acting as consultants or instructors or merely by answering a quick question by phone or letter, or by channeling bibliographic material to the student or the resource library once the student has returned home.

It is also important for graduating students to renew all memberships in professional organizations prior to their return home and to prepare change-of-address notifications so that future correspondence will be sent to them in their home countries. Returning students might also inquire as to the existence of local chapters of the organizations that they have joined, so that they might become active members upon returning to their home countries.

6.3.3. Upon return

Shortly after returning home, the graduate should visit his resource library in order to renew acquaintance with the librarian and to review the acquisitions made while he was away. If gaps in the collection are identified, the graduate should inform the library-information specialist immediately so that the needed material can be ordered, or an alternative means of acquiring the material can be investigated. Reviewing the collection in this way and ordering material in anticipation of future information needs will avoid delays when these needs arise.

Since the work carried out by the student studying abroad is probably related to local needs, a copy of the thesis or specialization paper should be donated to the library. In turn, the resource library should notify the national agency responsible for maintaining an index of theses and dissertations, if one exists, so that this information becomes available throughout the country.

The returned graduate might also want to notify the library-information specialists of materials acquired while abroad. If prior arrangements were made stipulating that materials acquired belong to the funding institution,

Developing a Resource Library

then the materials should be turned over to the resource library. If the bibliographic materials belong to the returning student, the library-information specialists should take note and consider ordering additional copies for the library. In any case, the library-information specialists should be aware of these materials, and they should be able to refer other users with similar interests.

On returning, the student should list his name and local address with the resource library and include a description of his specialty. The information provided to the resource library should be added to a directory, and the people listed will (1) be called upon as specialists or consultants, if needed; (2) talk to students who are considering studying abroad in the same institutions; or (3) participate in alumni groups or in meetings with graduates who have studied in other universities. In addition to submitting their own names to the directory, graduates might also list the names of specialists they met while abroad, assuming that the specialists were previously informed of the directory and had given permission. In the case of foreign specialists, the name of the contacting graduate student should also be included. If a directory of this sort does not exist in the home country, it may be necessary for the newly returned professional to take on the responsibility of developing and possibly maintaining this valuable tool.

6.3.4. An illustrative example

The example in this section presents the activities of a hypothetical student from country X who is planning to study for an advanced degree at a U.S. university. While various authors in the library-information science literature present different views as to the generalizability of conditions in developing countries (Lemos 1981), several problems involved with library and information resources seem to be present in all countries. These include rapid political change, lack of trained personnel, inadequate budgets, and collections that need to be improved and enlarged. These conditions were specifically reported to exist in Nigeria (Adimorah 1976) and in Latin American countries (Robredo 1976; Adams 1975).

The hypothetical student, a young man who wishes to study abroad, had been working at an electrical research center (ERC) for several years after having obtained a bachelor of arts degree in electrical engineering at the national university. The head of the division in which the young man works agreed that a master's or perhaps even a doctoral degree would be of benefit to the center, and he recommended that the young may be given a scholarship to study abroad. The scholarship was to be funded from two sources: the employer (ERC) and the Ministry of Education. While scholarships for study abroad are granted based on the needs of the country, financial conditions influence the number of scholarships granted. The young man applied for a scholarship. When his application was accepted by the funding sources for a scholarship and by a U.S. university, he was granted a leave of absence from the ERC to study abroad.

Before leaving for the United States, the young man identified available bibliographic resources in his home country, beginning with the library in the center where he worked. He learned that even the branch offices of the ERC, located in other parts of the country, have the necessary tools and communication links to inform employees of material available throughout the center.

The young man examined the card catalog by subject and scanned the reference collection. A quick look at the ERC's union catalog of periodicals revealed a number of relevant titles of both journals and indexing-abstracting services. The Union Catalog of Periodical Publications provided information on the holdings of various libraries in the country; however, the catalog had not been printed since 1976 so the holdings listed were outdated. The young man was pleased to learn of the bilateral agreement for exchanging technical reports between the ERC and an electric power research center located near the U.S. university where he intended to study. The ERC also has a computer terminal with access to databases, such as INSPEC (Information Services in Physics and Engineering Communities) and ISMEC (Information Service in Mechanical Engineering), among others. The librarians at the ERC recommended other library-informatation centers of interest to the young man, based on their experience in interlibrary loan and various directories available in the country.

After arriving in the United States, the student began to explore the available bibliographic resources at the university by attending the general orientation to the use of the library facilities offered at the beginning of each semester. He learned that various pamphlets are available about each of the libraries on campus, describing their subject specialties and indicating their locations and schedules. To gain additional knowledge of bibliographic and information resources as well as research methodology, he decided to take a course offered by the university's Graduate School of Library and Information Science called "Information Resources and Libraries." The student also wanted to explore available resources on his country and region of the world to keep up to date on happenings at home. He was able to enroll in another course offered at the university, on research resources in developing countries; the objective of the course is to acquaint students with general and specialized materials related to the home region. In the process of acquainting himself with the information services of the university, the student learned that his institution maintains a database on related activities in the United States and his own country. Although the information is quite limited, it is a valuable resource and the student can request additional information via the interinstitutional linkage through which the database has been developed.

Visits to the International House on campus provided an opportunity to make new friends and lessen feelings of isolation. The student also attended meetings and lectures at the International Center, where he had several opportunities to hear prominent guest speakers from his home region. Additional personal and professional contacts were made by joining a professional society for electrical and electronic engineers; the particular organization he chose to join has an international division, which enabled him to continue this affiliation after he returned home.

Approximately six months prior to completing his studies, the student contacted the library-information specialist at the ERC in a final effort to help obtain needed bibliographic materials. Once these items were identified, the student obtained the materials and shipped them home to avoid carrying large packages. The student had also made an effort throughout his studies to acquire appropriate materials for his personal library. Many of these materials had been received through his membership in the professional society and some had been collected at conferences, symposiums, and other meetings in his field. Because he began this practice early in his stay at the U.S. university, the student was able to collect a substantial amount of material at very low cost. Since much of the material was ephemeral and difficult to find in his own country, the bibliographic material will be particularly valuable.

When he returned home, the student visited the ERC library and was pleased to find that many of the books and journals that he had recommended while abroad were now included in the library collection. Two copies of the student's completed dissertation were submitted to the Ministry of Education and donated to the ERC library for use by other employees. The student also added the names of professional contacts he had made in the United States to the directory maintained by the library.

6.4. Conclusions

Library and information centers are important resources for students wishing to study abroad and for graduates returning from abroad. If students assume active roles in developing the collections at their local resource libraries, they will benefit greatly from these activities. Studying abroad provides students with access to a great variety of information resources, both bibliographic and personal, that can help enrich the local information centers. Therefore, before beginning their study abroad, students should familiarize themselves with local information resources so they can help improve collections for the benefit of themselves and others. Good library and information resources and continued use by professionals in developing countries will facilitate and improve the quality of the work and research performed.

Developing a Resource Library

The resource centers discussed in this chapter have been idealized, and in reality, they may exist only in embryonic form. Their development in many countries continues to be a slow process requiring the support and participation of everyone concerned, so that these resource libraries can, in the future, carry out their intended functions and be of great value to individual users and to the countries they serve.

References Cited

Adams, Scott. 1975. *Scientific and technical services in eight Latin American countries: Development, technical assistance, opportunity for cooperation.* Louisville, KY: University of Illinois, Urban Studies Center, NTIS PB-235 202/6WL.

Adimorah, E.N.O. 1976. Problems of scientific information work in developing countries. *The Information Scientist* (England) 10(4):139-148.

Asheim, Lester E. 1966. *Librarianship in developing countries.* Urbana: University of Illinois Press.

Herner, Saul, et. al. 1980. *A brief guide to sources of scientific and technical information.* Arlington, Va.: Information Resources Press.

Keren, C. and L. Harmon. 1980. Information services in less developed countries. In *Annual review of information science and technology,* vol. 15, pp. 289-324. Edited by Martha Williams. White Plains, N.Y.: Knowledge Industry Publications Inc.

Krevitt Eres, Beth. 1981. Transfer of information technology to less developed countries: A systems approach. *JASIS* 32(2):97-102.

Krzys, Richard, and Gaston Litton. 1975. Latin American librarianship. In *Encyclopedia of library and information science,* vol. 14, pp. 51-74. New York: Marcel Dekker.

Lemos, Antonio A. Briquet de. 1981. *A portrait of librarianship in developing societies.* Occasional Paper, no. 148. Urbana-Champaign, Ill.: University of Illinois Graduate School of Library and Information Science.

McCarthy, Cavan. 1975. Colonial cataloging. *New Library World* 77(March):55-56.

Robredo, Jaime. 1976. Problems involved in setting up and operating information networks in the developing countries. *UNESCO Bulletin for Libraries* 30(Sept./Oct.):251-254.

Saracevic, Tefko. 1980. Perception of the needs for scientific and technical information in less developed countries. *Journal of Documentation* 36(Sept.):214-167. Also *ERIC ED*-183 613.

Saracevic, Tefko, Gilda Maria Braga, and Alvaro Quijano Solis. 1979. Information systems in Latin America. In *Annual review of information science and technology*, vol. 14, pp. 249-282. Edited by Martha Williams. White Plains, N.Y.: Knowledge Industry Pub., Inc.

Shepard, Marietta Daniels. 1963. *An inter-American bibliographic institute: A proposal for comprehensive international bibliographic series and cataloguing control.* (Cuadernos Bibliotecologicas no. 16). Washington, D.C.: Organization of American States.

Slamecka, Vladimir, and Davis B. McCarn. 1979. *The information resources and services of the United States: An introduction for developing countries.* Washington, D.C.: International Science and Technology Institute, Inc. NTIS Report PB81-124737.

Wellisch, Hans. 1973. Linguistic and semantic problems in the use of English-language information services in non-English-speaking countries. *International Library Review* 5(2):147-162.

Bibliography

Boakari, Francis Musa. 1981. Relevance of U.S. education to the Third World: Challenges and satisfactions on returning home. *NAFSA Newsletter* 33(1):42-44.

Engineering Joint Council. 1979. *Program options through which the engineering profession of the U.S. can support the transfer of technology to LDCs.* New York: Engineering Joint Council. NTIS PB81-125445.

Herbert, W. 1981. Abroad in the U.S.: Foreign students on American campuses. *Educational Record* 62(Summer):68-71.

International student re-entry. 1981. *Colleges and Universities* 56(Summer): 418-419.

Laurhass, Ludwig, Jr. 1978. *Library resources on Latin America: Research guide and bibliographic introduction.* Los Angeles: UCLA Latin American Center and University Library.

Lyengar, T.K.S. 1977. *Developing countries and information needs and supply: A brief report of an international seminar.* Arlington, VA: ERIC. ED-176 757.

Neelameghan, A. 1978. Training of university students of engineering in the use of information. *Lib Sci Slant Doc* 15(December):201-203.

Okwvovulu, A.O. 1976. Biomedical periodicals in Nigerian medical libraries: The medical librarian's dilemma. *Bulletin. Medical Library Association* 64(3):305-308.

Slamecka, Vladimir. 1979. *Information transfer between the U.S. and developing countries: An assessment and suggestions.* Washington D.C.: International Science and Technology Institute, Inc. NTIS PB81-112542.

Vasudeva Rao, K.N. 1978. Training of practising engineers in information use. *Lib Sci Slant Doc* 15(December):199-200.

Vilentchuk, Lydia. 1975. *Guidelines on the conduct of a national inventory of scientific and technological information and documentation facilities.* Paris: UNESCO. SC-75/WS/28.

Bibliography on Collection Development

American Library Association. 1979. Resources and Technical Services Division. Collection Development Committee. *Guidelines for collection development*. Edited by David L. Perkins. Chicago: American Library Association.

Atherton, Pauline. 1978. *Handbook for information systems and services*. Paris: UNESCO.

Coleman, Kathleen, and Pauline Dickinson. 1977. Drafting a reference collection policy. *College and Research Libraries* 38(3):227-233.

Congrat-Butlar, Stefan. 1979. *Translation and translators: An international directory and guide*. New York: R.R. Bowker Co.

Directory of published proceedings, series SEMT-science/engineering/medicine/technology. 1965—. 10/year. volume 1-. White Plains, N.Y.: Interdok Corporation.

Dissertation Abstracts International B: The Sciences and Engineering. 1969—. Monthly. Ann Arbor, Mich.: University Microfilms.

Feng, Y.T. 1979. The necessity for a collection development policy statement. *Library Resources and Technical Services* 23(1):39-44.

Government Reports Announcements and Index. Vol 74. Bi-weekly. Springfield, Va.: U.S. Department of Commerce, National Technical Information Service.

Herner, Saul, et al. 1980. *A brief guide to sources of scientific and technical information*. Arlington, Va.: Information Resources Press.

Himmelsback, Carl J., and Grace E. Brociner. 1972. *A guide to scientific and technical journals in translation*. 2d ed. New York: Special Library Association.

Index Translationum. 1949—. Annual. Paris: International Institute of Intellectual Cooperation. 1932-40 n.s. Paris: UNESCO.

Lunsford, Effie B., and Theodore J. Kopkin. 1971. *A basic collection for scientific and technical libraries*. New York: Special Libraries Association.

Malinowsky, H. Robert, and J.M. Richardson. 1980. *Science and engineering literature: A guide to reference sources.* 3d ed. Littleton, Colo.: Libraries Unlimited.

Official Gazette of the United States Patent and Trademark Office. 1872—. Weekly. Annual Index. Washington, D.C.: U.S. Patent and Trademark Office.

Osburn, Charles B. 1979. Annual. Some practical observations on the writing, implementation and revision of collection development policy. *Library Resources and Technical Services* 23(1):7-15.

Scientific and Technical Books and Serials in Print. 1972—. New York: R. R. Bowker Co.

Shearer, Benjamin F., and Barbara Smith Shearer. 1981. *Finding the source: A thesaurus-index to the reference collection.* Westport, Conn.: Greenwood Press.

Sheehy, Eugene Paul. 1976. *Guide to reference books.* 9th ed. Chicago: American Library Association. Supplement II, 1982.

Smithsonian Science Information Exchange. 1978. *Information services on research in progress: A worldwide inventory.* Compiled in cooperation with UNESCO. Distribution by National Technical Information Service.

Spyers-Duran and Mann, ed. *Shaping library collections for the 1980s.* Oryx Press.

Subject Guide to Microforms in Print. 1978—. Annual. Westport, Conn.: Microform Review Inc.

Subject Guide to Books in Print. 1957—. Annual. New York: R. R. Bowker Co.

Ulrich's International Periodicals Directory: A Classified Guide to Current Periodicals Foreign and Domestic. 1932—. Biennial. New York: R.R. Bowker Co.

U.S. Superintendent of Documents. 1895—. Monthly. *Monthly Catalog of U.S. Government Publications.* Washington, D.C.: Government Printing Office.

Vertical File Index: Subject and Title Index to Selected Pamphlet Material. 1935—. Monthly, except August. New York: Wilson.

World Guide to Technical Information and Documentation Services. 1975. 2d ed. revised. Paris: UNESCO.

World Meetings Outside USA and Canada. 1968—. Quarterly. Newton Centre, Mass.: Technical Meetings Information Service.

7.

Continuing Education for the Returned Professional

Stephen C. Dunnett

7.1. Introduction

For developing countries, national development has always been one of the highest priorities in education. Training manpower, either at home or abroad, is usually related to national planning priorities in the major development areas of economic growth, public health, aid for rural and urban poor, and cultural development. National development, which today is viewed in both economic and social terms, has led to a great organized effort in higher education. This effort is manifest in many endeavors, from building national educational institutions to sending thousands of students abroad for training on all levels in a variety of fields. During the past twenty years, the rapid development of higher education at home and the return of professionals educated abroad has produced a very large number of specialists working in all sectors of the economies of developing countries.

During this same period of time, the modern world has undergone rapid technological, scientific, economic, and social change and development unparalleled in modern history. There is every indication that these changes, especially in the technological and economic areas, will proceed even more rapidly in the decades ahead. It is already clear that these developments have led to the emergence of new fields of knowledge and the rapid obsolescence of previous knowledge and old industries.

In developed countries, such as Japan and the United States, technological developments—particularly in computerization of information processing, transportation, medical technology, and energy—have resulted in a transformation of education and training for work. Projected trends in technology and science point to the need for increasingly specialized education. The emergence of the concept of a postindustrial society, which is knowledge-information intensive and thus economically successful, has led to the recognition that scientists, engineers, technicians, doctors, and teachers are the "workers" of the future. The demand for these knowledge-information workers requires a continuous investment in education and training, as well as in reeducation and retraining. Changes in occupational requirements have already produced wholesale and profound effects on all levels of the educational systems of developed countries. As workers and professionals attempt to keep abreast of technological changes, they will require retraining on a systematic basis, resulting in a constant reassessment of the way in which they are being educated for professional purposes.

Research in higher education indicates that only a small portion of the knowledge acquired by engineers, for example, during their university training is still useful five years after graduation. Managers in the corporate sector have long recognized that practical experience alone is no longer adequate to enable them to cope with the increasingly heavy demands of their jobs and the ever-changing conditions in which they work. Technical training that was acquired five to ten years ago in management is seldom relevant to the current conditions.

Recent surveys conducted in several developing countries have revealed that many returned university graduates do not work in their original fields of study. Furthermore, many returned graduates have indicated that the character of their jobs has changed at least once or twice during their careers. It is clear from these findings that university training cannot provide all the knowledge and expertise that professionals will need for the duration of their careers. The need for additional training to acquire new knowledge and expertise to cope with the ever-changing environment demands opportunities for continuing education throughout the professional's lifetime.

7.2. Professional Development Through Lifelong Learning

If professionals are to keep abreast of rapid change and development in their fields, as well as keep functioning at an adequate level of competence, they need lifelong learning opportunities. The terms "adult education," "lifelong learning," and "continuing education" are often used interchangeably to include all measures of planned learning for men and women after the statutory age for leaving school. The term continuing education usually denotes a stage beyond the basic acquisition of education. For the purposes of this discussion, it will be used to describe the process whereby a person who has acquired basic education undertakes sequential and organized activities with the conscious intention of bringing about changes in information, knowledge, understanding, skills, appreciations, or attitudes (adapted from *Exeter Papers* 1969).

In the United States, there is a long tradition of professional development through continuing education. It is estimated that some 50 million Americans are currently participating in some form of educational training for purposes of professional development. Their motivations are diverse and include hope of job advancement, a requirement to remain abreast of their fields, cultural interest, and community responsibilities. This broadly based interest in professional development may be related to the tradition of change and the responsibility of the individual to adapt to change that is deeply rooted in the development of the United States.

In a number of developing countries, providing training opportunities through continuing education is considered a major function of the education system. Fields such as medicine, teacher training, management, engineering, and agriculture have recognized this need and have worked closely with universities and professional societies to provide opportunities for professional development.

It is not easy to describe, let alone comprehend, all the variations of continuing education that exist in developing countries, nor is that the purpose of this chapter. It is obvious that the various models of continuing education that exist in the developing world are the result of national characteristics such as size, population, history, ideology, and the level of development of the educational system. Nevertheless, some general characteristics do exist, and most countries' models of continuing education do have features in common.

7.3. Models of Continuing Education

In developing countries, continuing education is sponsored mainly by government to train professionals employed in the public sector. In some countries, continuing education is directly tied to national socioeconomic planning. This is a result of the correlation between manpower planning and the planning of higher education. In other countries, there is no such coordinated planning, and continuing education is offered in a fragmented manner in response to current short-term industrial, economic, and social demands.

In the United States, by contrast, most continuing education opportunities have been provided by the nonpublic sector, that is, by private organizations, professional societies, and private corporations. Notable exceptions to this nonpublic approach are the extensive continuing education activities undertaken by state universities; the Co-Operative Extension Service (Agricultural Extension) with support from the federal, state, and county governments; and evening classes for adults in many public school systems throughout the United States (Harris 1980).

In both developed and developing countries, continuing education programs can range from one-day workshops or seminars to one-year, full-time, intensive certificate programs. Full-time programs are generally more efficient because participants can be trained quickly and in highly specialized fields. It is generally much easier to administer full-time programs, which can be tailored to meet local or even national needs. Needless to say, full-time programs are much more expensive and usually require the services of a full-time faculty.

Part-time programs are often more feasible in developing countries, not only because of the cost of operation, but also because it is easier for participants to take courses after working hours than to give up their jobs for a full-time program. Motivation is often higher in part-time programs since participants have an opportunity to apply their newly acquired skills in their daily work.

Faculty who teach in continuing education programs may be faculty members at local universities or professionals working in the field. In developing countries, in particular, there is a tendency to use newly returned professionals to assist in providing seminars, continuing education, and workshops to update other professionals in the same field. There are many other possibilities, of course. In some countries, newly returned professionals may very well become adjunct faculty members at local institutions of higher education and then teach others in continuing education programs. Certainly returned graduates should consider offering their services to their local universities both for the rewards to be obtained from assisting others and as an investment in their own future professional development.

Every professional field requires a very wide range of training experiences in continuing education on at least three levels: (1) highly technical and theoretical upgrading programs for individuals engaged full-time in that field, (2) brief orientation programs for beginners in the field or for middle-level technicians, and (3) training programs for those who lack basic skills in that profession, but who have considerable practical experience. Newly returned professionals who have been trained overseas can provide assistance in continuing education programs on all of these levels. In the future, they will themselves participate in technical and theoretical upgrading programs.

7.4. Summary

Continuing education, as defined here, consists of all the learning activities individual professionals participate in after the preparatory education that is necessary for entrance to the field. Learning experiences designated as continuing education are those designed primarily to increase the competence of practitioners in the performance of their professional duties.

Continuing education implies a concept of lifelong learning for professional development in order to meet the challenges of change and growth in the individual, as well as in the professional field and society at large. Continuing education includes those learning opportunities utilized by individuals in a particular profession which—

1. keep them up to date on new concepts, knowledge, and skills within the field and within related fields;
2. constantly update their basic educational training;
3. refresh them in various aspects of their basic education; and
4. prepare them for possible changes and new roles in their personal careers as a result of promotion, recycling, or other personal actions.

Professional development through continuing education is the personal responsibility of every professional. The individual must asume the basic responsibility for his own continuing education after graduation and return to the home country. Of course, if one views continuing education from a broader perspective, it does encompass the concern and shared responsibility of all members of the profession, the employing institutions, the academic institutions, professional societies, and the government of the country itself. The profession and institutions employing members of that profession have a responsibility to provide continuing education opportunities just as individual professionals have a responsibility to participate in them and an obligation to provide such opportunities to others.

7.5. Practical Suggestions for the Returning Professional

Professional development can take many forms and certainly goes beyond simply participating in continuing education programs after returning home. Professional development involves the professional's taking his place as a responsible and active member in his profession. It includes making every effort to be as competent as possible through proper training, study, and constant upgrading of his skills. There are a number of actions that can be taken prior to returning home that may prove helpful to future professional development. The following suggestions have been provided by students who have returned home after training in the United States. Prior to returning home, the student should—

1. join the U.S. or international professional societies and organizations in his professional field and related fields. These memberships should be maintained after return to the home country.

2. subscribe to useful professional journals that will keep him abreast of developments in his field.
3. develop a network of Americans and compatriots in his professional field. This may be accomplished in a number of ways, including joining his university's alumni association and even starting a chapter in his home country.
4. build up a strong reference library in his professional field to take home with him. It should be kept up to date with regular acquisitions after the return home.
5. identify and contact U.S. corporations, universities, and other institutions that may have exchange programs or other links with institutions in his home country.
6. identify and write to institutions of higher education in his home country that offer continuing education programs for professionals working in his field.

Once reestablished at home, returned professionals should—

1. contact local institutions of higher education, corporations, and government departments to determine what continuing education opportunities exist. If there are none, returnees should consider offering their services or starting their own U.S. alumni group.
2. contact the U.S. embassy or nearest U.S. consulate to find out what educational activities they offer. Returnees should offer to receive visiting American professionals in their fields.
3. return to the United States on a regular basis, if possible, to attend conferences and seminars of professional associations.
4. organize local, regional, national, and even international seminars and other meetings within their professional fields.
5. correspond with former teachers, advisers, and professional colleagues in the United States and elsewhere.
6. make an effort to keep up with the literature in their professional fields.
7. establish relations with foreign professionals in their fields resident in their countries.

Many returnees from study abroad complain of feeling isolated from international colleagues in their fields. Others complain of being out of touch with the latest developments and changes in their fields. But, conscious effort begun now and maintained after returning home will result in a richer and more productive professional career.

Major International and National Organizations in Continuing Education

International

Adult Education Division, Department of Elementary and Adult Education
  Ministry of Education
  Bangkok, Thailand

Adult Education National Committee
  c/o Ministry of Education
  Nouakchott, Mauritania

Adult Education National Committee
  c/o Assistant-Secretary General
    of the National Commission for UNESCO
  Ministry of Education
  Riyadh, Saudi Arabia

African Adult Education Association
  c/o Institute of Adult Education
  University of Ghana
  Legon, Accra, Ghana

  Arranges for research into problems of adult education in Africa; acts as a clearinghouse for information, publishes a journal, newsletter, and reports.

Asian Institute for Teacher Educators
  University of the Philippines
  Diliman, Quezon City, D-505, Philippines

Asian South Pacific Bureau of Adult Education
  c/o Indian Adult Education Association
  17B Indraprastha Marg
  New Delhi 1, India

  Publishes *Asian South Pacific Bureau of Adult Education Journal* and *Indian Journal of Adult Education.*

Australian Association of Adult Education
  Box 1346 P.O.
  Canberra City, A.C.T. 2601, Australia

Continuing Education

Comité National D'Education des Adultes
c/o Ministry of Education
Beirut, Lebanon

Council of Europe, Council for Cultural Cooperation
Committee for Out-Of-School Education and Cultural Development
Avenue de L'Europe
67 Strasbourg, France

Department of Adult Education
University of Ibadan
Ibadan, Nigeria

Division of Adult Education
UNESCO
Place de Fontenoy
757000 Paris, France

Jordanian National Committee for Adult Education
Ministry of Education
Amman, Jordan

Indian Adult Education Association
17B Indraprastha Marg
New Delhi 1, India

Institute of Adult Education
University of Dar-es-Salaam
P.O. Box 20679
Dar-es-Salaam, Tanzania

Interamerican Federation for Adult Education
Apartado 20.16 San Martin
Caracas, Venezuela

Coordinates and strengthens adult education associations in Latin America, publishes miscellaneous documents.

Literacy International
c/o Indian Adult Education Association
17B Indraprastha Marg
New Delhi 1, India

Conducts seminars, workshops, and conferences for professional literacy workers, provides an information and documentation service.

Continuing Education

National Education Council
 Ministry of Education
 Sultanate of Oman
 Muscat, Oman

National Institute of Adult Education
 25 Queen Street
 London W1M 0BL England

Regional Council for Adult Education and Literacy in Africa
 Permanent Secretary: P.N.A.
 Lome, Togo

Supreme Council for Adult Education
 Ministry of Education
 Cairo, Egypt

Supreme Literacy Board
 c/o Ministry of Education
 Baghdad, Iraq

UNESCO Institute for Education
 Feldbrunnenstrasse 70
 D-2000 Hamburg 13,
 Federal Republic of Germany

 Current activity centers on a long-range and comprehensive program of research and development and information on lifelong education.

World Conference of Organizations of the Teaching Profession
 Adult Education Commission
 5 Avenue de Moulin
 1110 Morges, Switzerland

 Composed of national, associate, and international organizations totaling 5 million teachers in 85 countries, publishes materials on various aspects of the teaching profession.

Zambia Adult Education Association
 P.O. Box RW 232
 Ridgeway, Lusaka, Zambia

Bibliography

Adult education. Washington, D.C.: Adult Education Society of the U.S.A. Published quarterly.

Adult education in Asia and the Pacific. 1982. Bangkok: UNESCO.

Adult education handbook. 1973. Dar-es-Salaam: Tanzania Publishing House.

Broadbent, D. 1971. Continuing education and retraining of engineers and technicians, *Journal of Engineering Education in Southeast Asia* 1.

Comparing adult education worldwide. Charters, Alexander N. and Associates. 1981. San Francisco: Jossey-Bass Publishers.

Directory of adult education documentation and information services. 1980. 2d ed. Paris: UNESCO. (IBEDOC reference series)

Directory of adult education periodicals. 1979. 6th rev. ed. Paris: Adult Education Section, Literacy, Adult Education and Rural Development Division, UNESCO.

Hall, Budd L., and Khatun Remtulla. 1973. *Adult education and national development.* Nairobi: East African Literature Bureau, English Press.

Harris, W.J.A. 1980. *Comparative adult education: Practice, purpose and theory.* New York: Longman, Inc.

Kulich, Jindra. 1972. *World Survey of Research in Comparative Adult Education: A Directory of Institutions and Personnel.* Toronto: Centre for Continuing Education at the University of British Columbia.

Liveright, A., and N. Haygood, eds. 1968. *The Exeter papers.* Report of the First International Conferences in the Comparative Study of Adult Education, Center for the Study of Liberal Education for Adults. Brookline, Massachusetts.

Lowe, J., ed. 1970. *Adult education and national building.* Edinburgh: Edinburgh University Press.

Muller, Josef. 1975. *Adult education and development with special reference to the Arab states.* Berlin: German Foundation for International Development.

National adult education boards, councils and other coordinating bodies. 1982. 4th ed. Paris: UNESCO.

Parkyn, F.W. 1973. *Towards a conceptual model of life-long education.* Paris: UNESCO.

Prosser, R., and R. Clarke. 1972. *Teaching adults: A handbook for developing countries.* Nairobi: East African Literature Bureau.

Townsend Coles, Edwin K. 1977. *Adult education in developing countries.* 2d ed. Elmsford, N.Y.: Pergamon Press.

8.

Conclusion

Mary Ann G. Hood

There are two fundamental ideas underlying the main focus of this volume. The first is that reentering the home country may involve a variety of personal, social, and professional problems for the returning student. The second is that, because much of the emphasis in the past several years has been on helping foreign students prepare for personal and social readjustment, the question of professional readjustment (professional integration) has been neglected or dealt with only in cursory fashion.

8.1. A Review: From Personal and Social Readjustment To Professional Integration

Preparation for going home, commonly called reentry or transition, is by no means a new or recent activity. A number of U.S. colleges and universities have been involved in preparation programs, as have other types of organizations, since at least 1959. Some of the early formally organized programs include the Michigan State University AID Communications Seminars, intended primarily for AID participant trainees; the Mohonk Consultations for foreign students; the Cincinnati Rotary Club's Going Home Seminars; the Beyond Cornell Seminars; the Summer Crossroads Programs in Colorado Springs, Colorado; and a variety of programs sponsored by the East-West Center in Hawaii. In general, these programs and others concentrated on the personal and social problems that might be encountered on the return home.

Conclusion

NAFSA's sponsorship of the 1974 Wingspread Colloquium on Reentry/Transition was an attempt to pull together the then-current experience and expertise in reentry-transition of foreign students. The colloquium resulted in a published report (Marsh 1975). This report did not stimulate any significant increase in program activity, but it did have the effect of heightening interest in the possibility of reentry-transition activities for foreign students. In June of 1976, NAFSA sponsored the National Leadership Training Seminar in reentry-transition programming. (An unpublished report on this seminar, also by Harriet Marsh, is available from NAFSA.) Subsequent to the National Leadership Training Seminar, there was some renewed interest in reentry-transition, but, on the whole, the seminar did not generate as much concern or program activity as was hoped for. What little programming did occur was concentrated on personal and social concerns: stimulating self-awareness and sensitivity to possible problems, thereby diminishing the seriousness of their impact on the individual.

The dearth of activity and research regarding reentry-transition, whether related to personal or professional concerns, is borne out by Spaulding and Flack (1976), who list only nineteen items under the rubric "returnees." But most of the sources investigated by Spaulding and Flack do not directly relate to reentry-transition concerns; rather, they relate to foreign students' perceptions of the usefulness of U.S. education and training. However, many of the working hypotheses listed in Spaulding and Flack strongly imply the need for far greater attention to reentry-transition concerns, particularly as those concerns relate to professional integration in the home country.

Despite the apparent lack of general interest in the problems that foreign students might face on return home, either in their personal or professional lives, the Agency for International Development, over the years, has shown its concern through a variety of endeavors. Throughout much of the 1960s, AID produced a number of evaluative reports on the training its sponsored students received in the United States and their subsequent reintegration after their return home. In the past few years, AID's interest in reentry has taken a different direction, as exemplified by its joint sponsorship with NAFSA of the Re-entry Seminar for AID-sponsored students (January 1981) and by its financial support for two recent studies.

With funding from AID, the American Association for Agricultural Economics (AAAE) conducted a study among foreign alumni who had studied agricultural economics at U.S. institutions. The purpose was to determine their attitudes about the usefulness of their studies, particularly as related to their professional careers. The results of the study appear in *Training agricultural economists for work in international development*, by Fienup and Riley (1980). None of the items in this survey specifically relates to reentry, but Fienup and Riley do point out that some respondents to the survey "said that the long absence from their countries had created re-entry

Conclusion

problems" (p. 82). Further, this study makes clear that returned professionals strongly desire continued contact with their U.S. institutions and assistance in developing professional networks in their home countries.

Based on a survey of several hundred foreign students studying in various U.S. institutions, Motoko Lee published a study, *Needs of foreign students from developing nations at U.S. colleges and universities*, in 1981. Like the AAAE study, the Lee study was funded by AID. Of the approximately 175 items in the survey questionnaire, 14 were devoted to reentry concerns. Specifically, they relate to the logistics of returning home and to professional concerns after the return to one's country; none was related to personal or social concerns. From this study, one may conclude that foreign students do have legitimate anxieties and questions about packing up and returning home after a lengthy stay in the United States; more important, many of them are concerned about finding jobs, about finding positions appropriate to their training, about opportunities in their own countries that will contribute to their professional growth, about the facilities and equipment that they will have—or not have—to work with, and about continued contact with their U.S. institutions and with professionals in their disciplines.

In NAFSA's report on the Fourth AID/NAFSA Workshop, *The relevance of U.S. education to students from developing countries* (Jenkins 1980), there is a clear call for more predeparture workshops on reentry-transition and management "to assist in re-adjustment and use of knowledge gained." Such recommendations have come not only from professionals working in international educational exchange, but also from foreign students themselves. Student participants in the UDC Global Education Conference (November 1979) asked for "more efforts towards keeping students in touch with their home countries...and preparing them for the reality of re-entering the Third World...." Student participants in the 1978 NAFSA-sponsored Workshop for International Women Students—Women in Development—urged the following kinds of activities, particularly for female foreign students: workshops aimed at helping female foreign students better learn how to put their newly acquired skills to use in their home countries, guidelines and checklists for reentry problems and concerns, reentry programs for female foreign students, and the development of a support network designed especially to help female foreign alumnae keep in touch with their institutions and with each other. A major conclusion to be drawn from this particular workshop is that the problems facing women in their return home are far greater than those facing male students. (This point is admirably underscored by Pigozzi, Barnes-McConnell, and Williams in chapter 4.) A similar conclusion was reached in 1979 by Pamela Stevens, based on a survey of female foreign students at two universities in the Southeast.

More recently, student participants in the January 1981 seminar for AID-sponsored students, "Re-entering the Home Culture," were suffi-

Conclusion

ciently impressed by the seminar's program, concentrating on the professional aspects of reentry, that nearly 80 percent of them said they would share some of what they had experienced in the course of the seminar with their campus and university colleagues. A number of them specifically asked for more such seminars and for broad dissemination of the seminar report as a stimulus for further discussion and activity.

8.2. Professional Integration

The foregoing suggests a shift in emphasis regarding reentry: from major attention to the personal and social problems that one must cope with on returning home to those matters that affect the foreign student in terms of his professional and career concerns. This does not mean that the personal and social focus is unwarranted, but, rather, that there are other critical factors to be taken into account, that is, professional concerns. The Lee study, in particular, makes this point, and it includes the following strong recommendation: "...we contend that U.S. educational institutions and [the U.S.] government, in conjunction with the students' home governments, need to better plan and ensure that students be given appropriate professional opportunities and facilities to utilize their training and further advance their knowledge upon returning to their home countries" (Lee 1981, p. 132).

This volume, then, is an attempt to respond to the various calls for greater emphasis on the professional aspects of returning home, professional integration. In this spirit, the authors of the various chapters share advice that they believe is practical and workable in situations that may be far different from those encountered on the campuses of U.S. institutions and in the communities surrounding those campuses. Not everything suggested in this book will work in all instances, and, certainly, none of the authors believes that his ideas and suggestions will solve all the professional problems the returning student may face. Further, while each of the chapters deals with its own separate and distinct issues, all of them recommend that the student—

- bear in mind that he will return home at some point, and consciously plan for that return:
- maintain contact, while in the United States, with his peers and professional colleagues;
- maintain contact with the U.S. institution from which he graduated;
- be persistent in maintaining that contact;
- seek out and establish contact with professional peers in the home country;

Conclusion

- contribute to the advancement of science and knowledge in the home country, especially through research and publication;
- seek ways of continuing his professional growth; and
- fulfill the obligation of being a resource for others who may go abroad to study, after he has returned home.

Clearly, as the contributors to this volume have pointed out, adhering to these principles is not an easy task and, in fact, requires the foreign student's constant dedication and willingness to continue despite the frustrations that he might encounter. However, the task will be less burdensome if the foreign student can depend on faculty and other members of the university community to fulfill a concomitant obligation.

Just as there are principles by which the foreign student can better prepare himself for smoother professional integration, so are there principles by which we who work with foreign students in U.S. colleges and universities must be guided. It matters little that the returned foreign student tries, repeatedly, to maintain contact with departmental faculty and advisers if such attempts are met with indifference or nonresponse. If faculty, advisers, administrators, and the institution's support staff and services are to assist in meaningful ways in the process of professional integration, they must—

- respond sensitively and sensibly with appropriate and caring advice and guidance;
- help the student focus on the problems and prospects of his own country in the classroom, in the laboratory, and in his research efforts;
- encourage the U.S. institution to pay more active attention to foreign alumni, not only at the departmental level, but also at the institutional level (alumni services offices and career or placement offices);
- make a conscious effort to keep in touch with returned students;
- serve as consultants or resource persons, even though the task may be complicated (because it is to be carried out abroad), and even though it may offer little financial compensation; and
- take the time to seek out former students and to offer their services, should the occasion for foreign travel or assignment arise.

8.3. Areas for Further Cooperation and Research

All of the chapters in this book suggest or imply areas for further cooperation and research in building a supporting infrastructure for the profes-

Conclusion

sional integration of returning foreign students. The suggestions include the following:

- establishing alumni networks (Rogers in chapter 2),
- establishing professional networks (Moravcsik in chapter 3),
- establishing women's networks (Pigozzi et al. in chapter 4),
- establishing research support networks (the Lees in chapter 5),
- improving library systems in developing countries (Borko and Goldstein in chapter 6), and
- developing alternatives for continuing education opportunities (Dunnett in chapter 7).

I would like to suggest that the following might contribute to the process of professional integration and, at the same time, make more readily achievable part of the professional infrastructure advocated by all the contributors to this volume.

Several of the chapter authors, particularly Borko and Goldstein, the Lees, and Moravcsik, point out the difficulties surrounding research and publication in developing countries. One of the major reasons for this state of affairs would appear to be the lack of information about what has been done and what might be possible. A step toward increasing the amount of information available might be to do what Osman Hassan Ahmed did. Ahmed, former cultural counselor at the Embassy of the Sudan, spent several years compiling information on theses and dissertations written by Sudanese students in the United States, Canada, and the Caribbean, as well as information on theses and dissertations about Sudan written by non-Sudanese students. The result is a remarkable bibliography: *Sudan and Sudanese: A bibliography of American and Canadian dissertations and theses on the Sudan* (1982).

In the process, the Embassy of the Sudan has acquired, since 1977 when the policy for acquisition was established, two copies of each master's thesis or doctoral dissertation produced by a Sudanese student studying in the United States or Canada. As Ahmed says in the introduction to his bibliography, "The primary benefit...is to make available a data base for research in education, cultural exchange, manpower training, brain drain, etc., on Sudan." One copy of each thesis and dissertation is retained by the embassy in Washington, D.C., and the second is sent to the library at the University of Khartoum in the Sudan for the benefit of users of that library.* Such a policy doubles the usefulness of the database, since the

---

*I am indebted to Mrs. Janice Ezeani, who worked with Osman Hassan Ahmed for many years on the bibliography project, for confirming that copies of acquired theses and dissertations are sent to Khartoum.

Conclusion

material is available for researchers, students, and professionals in the Sudan, as well as in the Sudanese Cultural Affairs Office in Washington, D.C.

This kind of project may also have been undertaken by other embassies of developing countries, or such a project may be in process, though I am unaware of any such effort. Certainly, it would make sense to encourage similar projects by embassies or governmental agencies of other developing countries. In any case, this type of compiled information might be useful to returning students in several ways. It could serve—

- to suggest the names of professional colleagues with whom one might establish contact,
- to provide information on the specializations and research interests of one's fellow countrymen, and
- to form the foundation of a collection of materials on a particular country for a repository library in that country.

An additional effort suggests itself here: translation of theses and dissertations, or, at the very least, dissertations, into the common language of educated discourse in the home country. Assuredly, it may be time consuming and difficult to undertake such a translation project, but it would be worthwhile in broadening the base of possible professional contacts and increasing opportunities for further cooperative research endeavors.

In chapter 3, Moravcsik suggests that the returned professional make use of any existing ham radio network in his home country. Radio might very well serve scientists and scholars in other ways, including broadcasting conferences and continuing education projects.

The Education Department of the World Bank began a study of the use of radio for educational purposes in 1975. The results of that study appear in *Alternative routes to formal education: Distance teaching for school equivalency* (1982). In general, this report is concerned with the use of radio broadcasts to achieve primary and secondary school equivalency. Nevertheless, two of the chapters may have some relevance here. One chapter describes inservice training broadcasts for teachers in Kenya, and a second chapter describes some quite successful radio programming by Everyman University in Israel. Everyman University, patterned after the British Open University, offers both academic and adult education courses.

This study of the use of radio broadcasting in education makes very clear that distance teaching or educational radio has certain disadvantages and that it is not always cost effective. However, short-term programming for very specific purposes, in particular, might well be a partial solution to some of the difficulties in arranging short updating courses or professional conferences and meetings, especially those difficulties related to distance,

Conclusion

time, and the high cost of planning and implementing such courses and meetings. In countries where there is a well-established and widespread radio network, it would seem reasonable to investigate the possibility of using it for continuing professional activities.

8.4. A Final Note

In both the immediate and the more distant future, the process of smooth professional integration in a developing country will depend more on the individual returning student's determination and capacity for creativity than it will on any set of "how to" guidelines. The ideas advocated by the contributors to this volume will be useful only to the extent that these ideas are carefully examined, adapted to fit a particular situation, and tentatively tried out and modified as needed. And however useful or helpful these ideas may or may not be, they cannot be improved upon if returned students do not communicate with the authors and with faculty and advisers in the U.S. institutions where they have studied. As Moravcsik so eloquently elaborates in chapter 3, continuing communication and interaction are vital to the world community of scientists, scholars, and professionals.

References Cited

Ahmed, Osman Hassan. 1982. *Sudan and Sudanese: A bibliography of American and Canadian dissertations and theses on the Sudan.*

Fineup, Darrell F., and Harold M. Riley. 1980. *Training agricultural economists for work in international development.* Washington, D.C.: American Agricultural Economics Association.

Jenkins, Hugh M. 1980. *A report on the fourt AID/NAFSA workshop: The relevance of U.S. education to students from developing countries.* Washington, D.C.: NAFSA.

Lee, Motoko Y. 1981. *Needs of foreign students from developing nations at U.S. colleges and universities.* Washington, D.C.: NAFSA.

Marsh, Harriet. 1975. *Re-entry/transition seminars: Report on the Wingspread colloquium.* Washington, D.C.: NAFSA.

Spaulding, Seth, and Michael J. Flack. 1976. *The world's students in the United States: A review and evaluation of research on foreign students.* New York, New York: Praeger Publishers.

World Bank. 1982. *Alternative routes to formal education: Distance teaching for school equivalency.*